WHERE HAD HE COME FROM?

They backtracked him on the north slope, which was covered with deep snow because it received little sun. Cronin worked his way down beside the tracks for several hundred yards . . . the visitor had evidently strode up that declivity; his prints seemed to come from over the edge of the earth, up out of the valley far below. He must have been as strong as a gorilla, or stronger . . .

THE YETI . . .
WAS HE FANTASY OR FACT,
STRANGER THAN FICTION?

IN SEARCH OF
MYTHS AND MONSTERS

by Alan Landsburg

FOREWORD BY LEONARD NIMOY

BANTAM BOOKS · TORONTO · NEW YORK · LONDON

RLI: $\dfrac{\text{VLM 9 (VLR 8–10)}}{\text{IL 9+}}$

IN SEARCH OF MYTHS AND MONSTERS
A Bantam Book | July 1977

ISBN 0-553-11137-X

Published simultaneously in the United States and Canada

Bantam Books are published by Bantam Books, Inc. Its trade-
mark, consisting of the words "Bantam Books" and the por-
trayal of a bantam, is registered in the United States Patent
Office and in other countries. Marca Registrada. Bantam
Books, Inc., 666 Fifth Avenue, New York, New York 10019.

PRINTED IN THE UNITED STATES OF AMERICA

To *Leonard Nimoy*
who understands the true
nature of strange phenomena
and whose diligent efforts
inspire all of the searchers

ACKNOWLEDGMENT

To Keith Monroe, my editorial associate, who makes sure that the ideas unearthed by the *In Search of . . .* film crews are organized into readable literature.

AUTHOR'S NOTE

The chronicle of discovery amassed in this volume is the work of many people. More than one hundred researchers, scientists, and skilled film-makers participated in the various quests. For simplicity's sake we have commingled our experiences into a single first-person narrative so that we may share with you the essence and excitement of the hunt without a clutter of personal introductions. As author and chief chronicler of this work, I owe an enormous debt of gratitude to those who joined me in the field to explore the world of mystery. To all those dedicated workers committed to *In Search of . . .* I say thank you. This book is as much yours as mine.

Alan Landsburg

Foreword by
LEONARD NIMOY

My first working association with the television series *"In Search of . . ."* was a narration session in which I was asked to read aloud the major objectives of the various categories—lost civilizations, strange phenomena, missing persons, magic and witchcraft, myths and monsters, and finally extraterrestrials. The role call of subjects was mind-bending. I kept on reading the sentences appended to the list but my mind was focused on the prospect of walking the electrifying path between known scientific fact and far-out science fiction.

Alan Landsburg is a much honored producer of television documentary films, and his extraordinarily talented staff of directors, writers, cameramen, and editors was out in the field collecting some of the most unusual images ever recorded for television. What appealed to me most was the very range of subjects. On the one hand we might be searching for Amelia Earhart, lost on a trans-Pacific flight in 1937; on the other, for the famed Count Dracula of myth and fact. Who built Stonehenge? Where do UFOs land? Is there really life after death? Do plants speak? The quest and the questions presented virtually an unlimited source of adventure. More than a hundred people were scattered around the world recording data, clues, evidence that fulfilled Hamlet's promise that "there are more things on earth than you have dreamed of in your philosophy."

I liked the sense of butting up against old ideas and

demonstrating that new explanations were possible. In pursuit of old baffling mysteries, the programs opened new directions to pursue in search of more illuminating answers. For all these reasons I immersed myself in the fascinating game. It's good to know that our television series *"In Search of . . ."* has now become something of a byword for many viewers.

This book is a chronicle of the efforts that have gone into making the series. It's a fascinating logbook to me, filled with the excitement of overcoming the impossible and the fulfillment of discovery. I hope you find it as intriguing as I did.

Leonard Nimoy

Contents

1

Monsters and I

I've come to know that things aren't always what they seem.

This gives me a burning curiosity that I can indulge, because I'm in the business of producing television documentaries. Whenever I get curious about something that may be but probably isn't, I go in search of it. If it actually is, I get footage for one of my shows.

Often the search is a tortuous voyage, through crosscurrents and dark whirlpools where myth and science and rumor converge and scatter and merge again. History and nature are full of surprises.

Last year I got curious about monsters.

I knew that certain supposedly mythical monsters had turned out to be soundly rooted in natural history. And I kept picking up vibrations about others. I caught hints that solid facts lay beneath some of yesterday's superstitions and today's tall tales.

I grew curious enough to do some preliminary reading and interviewing. I netted a hodgepodge of notes about monsters, pseudomonsters, nonmonsters, paramonsters, and others.

I began to sort them out so that I could investigate seriously. First, I asked myself, what is a monster?

In modern English we use the word in two very different senses. Commonly it means either "something of remarkable size"—even a monster cabbage or a monster wedding cake—or "a creature of peculiar savagery," which we likewise use hyperbolically more often than literally; that is, children tend to be called little monsters unless they are little angels.

I wasn't curious about figurative monsters. I wanted to track creatures that were monsters in the older, darker, more exact sense of the word.

The Romans, who invented the word *monstrum,* classed monsters with omens and prodigies; all were warnings sent by the gods, and hence were considered vaguely supernatural. The birth of a legless pig or hunchback son—a typical monster as they meant the word—was considered a warning to its owner or parent to make a ritual sacrifice to fend off disaster. The colt foaled on Julius Caesar's farm with each hoof divided into five toes was called a monster; but Caesar determined to make it an evil sign for the enemies of Rome rather than for himself, so he broke it in, and rode it to victory after victory.

The practical Romans were skeptical, as most Americans are, of mythical monsters. The poet Horace, for example, poked fun at such "unnatural" forms as centaurs and satyrs, never realizing that eyewitness tales of them were more or less truthful. Witnesses had seen Pelasgian Greek tribes who disguised themselves as horses and goats in ritual dances.

Similarly, the Incas and Aztecs, who had never seen horses, much less men on horseback, were horrified by the invading Spaniards' cavalry; they thought that man and horse were one. When a rider fell, the warriors fled in panic, thinking that somehow a monster had split into two creatures. Similar optical illusions might lie at the root of Greek mythology's half-human half-horse Chiron, the centaur.

Years ago I found that the mythical bull-man Minotaur, whom Theseus the Greek slew in a sacred labyrinth on Crete, stood for the king of Knossos while, perhaps, he impersonated the Semitic bull-god El. How many other myths of brutish phantasms arose similarly from facts? This was something I wanted to look into.

I knew that such unlikely mythological monsters as the unicorn and the chimera were also proved long afterward to be less fanciful than the Romans had assumed. The unicorn (the one-horned horse) was supposed to have dwelt in faraway regions where, we now know, the one-horned rhinoceros flourished; travelers had seen it, and their descriptions got blurred with the passage of generations.

The chimera? The word is still used in English to mean an illusory fancy or a wild incongruous notion. Most scholars agree that the chimera is "the one creature that seems most likely to have started only in man's imagination," as Daniel Cohen wrote in his blithe book *A Modern Look at Monsters*.

Yet Homer, who recorded that this monster lived in Asia Minor and breathed flames, suffered no chimerical delusions. Myths always described the chimera identically, and always localized it; it was always composed of a lion, a goat, and a snake, and it vomited fire, and it always ravaged in the mountains of woody Lycia.

Classical prose writers portrayed the phenomenon of the chimera with curious accuracy, as it turned out later. Seneca wrote, "In Lycia is a remarkable region. The ground is perforated in many places; a fire plays harmlessly without any injury to growing things." Strabo explained, "The neighborhood is the scene of the fable of the chimera, and at no great distance is Chimaera, a sort of ravine." Servius knew the geographical underpinning of the myth. He specified, "The flames issue from the summit of Mount Chimaera. There are lions in the region under the peak. The middle parts of the hills abound with goats, and the lower with serpents."

There the matter rested until, at the end of the last century, a British admiral named Beaufort anchored off Lycia on hydrographic work. Every night he saw flames on a mountaintop. Natives told him it had always burned. He climbed the mountain and found flames of natural gas spouting from crevices. The ancient Phoenician word *Chamirah* means "burning mountain." I could see how, as Greek settlements spread over Lycia, the meaningless Phoenician names were retained like Indian names in America, and how the tale trickled back to the Greek homelands of a strange mountain called Chamira, from which flames escaped, and then of a monster Chimaera with its lions and goats and snakes, ravaging in the mountains of Lycia. And so the story was finally fitted for the manipulation of Greek poets, who made stout Bellerophon kill the chimera, never dreaming they sent him on a quixotic tilt against a burning gas well.

The Old English word for an abnormal creature was *baeddel,* something that boded ill, from which our word *bad* comes. Thalidomide babies are typical *baeddels,* or monstrous births; they convey a warning against rash scientific experiment and against using a drug without knowing all its possible effects. I have heard rumors that the warning is still disregarded in certain so-called advanced scientific laboratories, and that monstrous creatures might be spawned there. There is a school of thought that suggests that sexual intercourse may not be the ideal means for human propagation. It sees big advantages (and may be cavalier about the risks) in laboratory fertilization of selected donor eggs and sperm, the cloning of cells taken from chosen individuals, and the use of other extraordinary procreative biotechnologies. I decided to follow this up too.

For my purposes, the key characteristics of a monster were mystery and menace. So I would go wherever there might be truth behind tales of mysterious menacing creatures—even human beings, if there were something truly monstrous about them, such as the werewolves and vampires of European folklore. This might include the ogres described in storybooks; I knew there were detailed descriptions of human giants in the Bible and in Roman histories.

I wanted to investigate present-day rumors of wild hairy giants hiding in swamps and mountain fastnesses. Do such things really exist? If so, could they be descended from Behemoth, the ill-defined monster in the Book of Job? Or might they be a form that primeval man once knew and competed with, then forced to seek refuge in places where men seldom went?

Two million years ago we weren't men. One million years ago we were. But our cultural evolution has apparently been packed into the last twelve thousand years or so. Why should it take so much longer for an ape to become man than for a caveman to become an Einstein?

There are huge gaps in the record. Surely there's more to our history than the meager chronicles of a few millennia. I've long suspected that our religious beliefs, our folklore, and our old superstitions are the detritus of earth's lost history. Perhaps researchers into the old monster stories—and even the new monster stories—are raising tiny corners of the veil that shrouds our distant past. I determined to talk with those researchers; to journey onto whatever frail bridges to the past they might be building.

One of the foremost of these researchers was Loren Eiseley, the great anthropologist and author. Remarks in an essay of his set me thinking:

> More than ninety per cent of the world's animal life of past periods is dead. Though it flourished in some instances longer than the whole period of human development, somewhere along its evolutionary path it vanished without descendants, or it was transformed, through still mysterious biological processes, into something else. . . .

> We can't trace the living races far into the past. We know little or nothing about why man lost his fur. . . . Though theories abound, we know little about why man became man at all.

> We know as little about some other missing creatures from the geological record. Why, for example, do bats hurl themselves so suddenly upon us, fully formed, out of the Paleocene era? They bear a distant relationship to ourselves. How they became bats and not men is one of those problems which involve the interplay of vast and ill-understood forces. . . .

The number of forms and datings suggest . . . a variety of early man-apes, not all of whom had necessarily taken the final step of becoming human.

Maybe Dr. Eiseley's "missing creatures from the geological record" included the Abominable Snowman of the Himalayas, the legendary Sasquatch and Bigfoot of our own Pacific Northwest, and the rumored monster-men in vast Southern swamps.

I already knew that various large mammals had shown remarkable ability in escaping documentation by scientists. The mountain gorilla, the pigmy hippopotamus, the white-haired snow monkey, and the giant panda were all well known to native villagers, yet they remained unknown to science for decades. The kouprey, a large wild bison, wasn't discovered by Western science until 1936, when the first specimen was identified at the Paris zoo. This beast roams the open savanna and woodland areas of Cambodia, where the terrain leaves it highly visible. But zoologists, quick as they are to accept fossil evidence, usually deride eyewitness reports of large unclassified creatures that appear only briefly. So who knows what undiscovered giants may come slithering out of the dark someday, just as the terrible giant squid (described in myths as Scylla) arose from ocean depths to confound experts who had always insisted it was merely mythical?

In fact, science now admits that there are creatures all around us that should have been extinct aeons ago. The turtle, the alligator, the horseshoe crab, some snails, a few of the spiders and cockroaches, and all the snow fleas have remained unchanged by evolution over millions of years.

Conversely, certain large species died off, we think, when there seemed no reason for their deaths. If there was no reason for them to die out, may not some have survived?

As an example of how uncertain we are, consider the horse. Horses evolved in North America. Rocks contain a complete record of their evolution. But then at the end of the Pleistocene period of the Ice Age,

horses disappeared from North American fossil findings. The horses' habitat obviously didn't disappear
when the horses did. Why then did horses die out in
the first place? Or did they? When they "reappeared,"
had they really been roaming unseen during the long
interim?

My point is that many other creatures, some monstrous, are said to have died out simply because later
strata show no traces of them.

But of course all strata aren't available for inspec-
tion, and there's no law that says a living species has
to leave any fossils at all. So I'm willing to consider
the possibility that there are still large, unknown, and
truly monstrous creatures alive in the world.

In the nineteenth century zoologists heard reports of
an amazing curiosity, which, as usual, they refused to
believe. Australians claimed to have found a hairy
creature that produced milk (through mammary glands
that lacked nipples) yet laid eggs! Even when the zoologists were shown specimens of the nonesuch (dead,
unfortunately, because it can't live outside its natural
habitat) they turned away, growling "Clumsy fraud."
The creature had a bill and webbed feet, obviously
impossible for a hairy milk giver. Nevertheless, a place
eventually had to be made for it in the recognized
animal kingdom, and a name given to it. The duck-
billed platypus lives.

The dodo lived too. It dwelt happily on the island
of Mauritius, in the Indian Ocean. It was a sort of
oversized dove, so fat that its wings couldn't lift it.
Arab traders in their dhows called at the island, but
didn't disturb the peaceful creatures. When Western
man arrived in the sixteenth century, however, hunters
soon made the dodo the first species in recorded history that clearly became extinct through human agency. By the nineteenth century, zoologists were saying
that it probably never existed, even though paintings
of it hung on walls of Mauritian homes. Only when
large numbers of dodo bones were found did science
accept their existence.

In 1952 something was dredged alive from the ocean

depths. It was small, but repulsive enough to be called
monstrous, and it was unknown to science, which christened it *Neopilina*. This slimy invertebrate was neither
a worm nor a snail, but the experts finally realized that
both must be offshoots of it.

These stories prove that zoology isn't a static science. The days of discovery aren't over yet. In fact,
nature may be creating monstrous new creatures almost under our eyes. In Florida, catfish began walking
in 1967, and have done so ever since; they are often
seen trundling across highways and lawns, using their
stubby but muscular pectoral fins. They can live out
of water for hours. Some can even climb trees.

On the wild, glacial, windswept peninsulas of Norway, stories are current of other creatures considered
impossible by science: giant sea serpents, or at least
huge things with reptilian heads and serpentine necks.
If they exist, they may be monsters out of the primeval
slime, gratefully thought long extinct—or they may be
something new, some mutation.

There is similar talk along the shores of very deep,
sky-high lakes in Scotland and Ireland and the far
northern countries. Down at the bottom of those lakes,
something big may live amid the oozes in the perpetual
darkness, and may surface occasionally. There are vast
wastes of unexplored deep water in the seas as well as
in mountain lakes. Who knows what is evolving there,
or what may be living there unchanged since the age
of the dinosaurs? I wanted to know, or at least examine the known clues.

The talk of serpentine sea giants put me in mind of
dragons. The Greek word *drakon* means just "serpent." Of course the dragon is the archetypal monster
of all times and all countries. What sets it above other
monsters is the widespread belief in it.

To Christian theologists the dragon is the embodiment of evil. When the archangel Michael cast evil out
of heaven, it was a dragon that he ejected, as told in
Revelations: "The great dragon was cast out, that old
serpent called the Devil." Saint George, patron saint
of England, who allegedly liberated his countrymen by

killing a dragon, may well be a Christianized version of the Babylonian god Marduk, who similarly killed a sea serpent, the malign goddess Tiamat. Pope John XXIII, presumably aware that the slaying of the sea serpent had been attributed to Jehovah himself by the prophet Isaiah, demoted George in the historical hierarchy of saints but allowed his worship to continue in places where he was particularly venerated.

To medieval Christians, the dragon was more than an allegorical personification of evil. It was as real as the wolf and the bear. Even in the seventeenth century, scholars wrote learned descriptions of dragons, and classified them in reference works among other types of serpents.

The lizard type of dragon came from China. Chinese travelers had seen gigantic lizards on the East Indian island of Komodo (where these creatures still grow to twelve-foot lengths) and brought back reports that became legends. The dragon was the premier mythological animal of the Orient as well as Europe. Similarly, various dragonlike troglodytes are described in the folklore of pre-Columbian North and South America, and of Africa.

I wanted to find out what creature inspired this powerful, shimmering phenomenon of worldwide imagination. Was there a living model for the dragon legends? Why was it a symbol of overpowering evil?

Dr. Edgar Dacque, a geology professor at the University of Munich, pointed out that millions of years ago there was a whole host of colossal beasts as dreadful as any the mind of man could invent: the numerous species of dinosaurs. Beside these, the mythical dragon looks almost tame. Dr. Dacque wondered—as did I—if some of these prehistoric monsters might have survived into the dawn of *Homo erectus*. Once seen, such terrifying monsters wouldn't easily be forgotten. They might haunt men's campfire tales and nightmares for generations, so the memory might be preserved through space and time from the last haunt of the dinosaur itself.

Maybe the remembrance gave form to the image of

the dragon atop Babylon's great Ishtar Gate. It was a scaly, high-legged monster with a long neck. Or maybe this was more than a memory: according to tradition, the Babylonians actually kept a dragon, which they worshiped as a god. From what we know of natural history, this seems highly unlikely. But as I said in the beginning, experience in odd corners of the world has taught me that things aren't always what they seem.

If there never were dragons, why did the thought of an imaginary one seem so evil and terrifying to civilizations already old before the Bible was written?

What gave anyone the idea for the griffin, the basilisk, and other animals that we now feel sure were imaginary? What caused people to believe in the existence of these in the first place? Sheer credulity? Or was there evidence? (Like the evidence that finally proved the roc, giant bird of the Arabian Nights, to be a reality.)

And why had so many people believed in composite half-human mixtures like mermaids, harpies, phoenixes, and sphinxes?

Why do some forms of life die out while others survive for millions of years? What causes a change in the genetic code of a species? We know now that we can change this inheritance code in the laboratory. Can we also create life—create monstrous living hybrids?

The questions were buzzing thick and fast in my mind. I was ready to go see for myself what answers were at hand.

2

The Reign of the Monsters

The fight was more fierce than anything ever seen by man.

Ready to attack, a monster lurked in the steaming underbrush, watching with small greedy eyes. He was like a thing out of nightmare. His short forelegs had claws like meathooks; his enormous jaw was lined with teeth as long as butcher's knives. In the far future he would be called tyrannosaur, and described as the biggest killer ever to stalk the earth. His food was the living flesh of other dinosaurs.

Suddenly he reared up kangaroo-fashion on massive hindquarters and tail. He towered as high as a two-story building. With a roar, he crashed through the trees toward his prey.

The prey was even more monstrous—as long as a basketball court and almost as wide. Man would name this creature brontosaur, from the Greek for "thunder lizard." At seventy thousand pounds, she outweighed her attacker three to one. The brontosaur was a water-based creature, so she was vulnerable now, and tried to scuttle toward deep water and safety. She had been grazing in the swamp grass, munching the several hundred pounds of plant food she needed daily.

She left footprints as big as bathtubs in the slime as she trundled along. The pursuing carnivore was gaining on her, his powerful rear legs propelling him at a speed of at least thirty miles per hour.

His front claws were ready like hands to clutch and

rip. But his first rush failed. The brontosaur lashed her massive trailing tail, and hit him so hard that he was knocked down into the brush.

He quickly charged again.

Once more the tail—which even at its tip was as thick as a telephone pole, and almost as hard—slammed him sideways. As he sprawled, his hooked eight-inch talons raked open the brontosaur's flank.

The duel went on; the wounded giantess struggled toward the lagoon, where deep water would buoy her bulk. Another sweep of her only weapon, her tail, made her enemy stumble a third time. But then the tail, which was activated by a kind of second brain in her spinal cord near her hips, could not lash back fast enough. The predator's renewed rush carried him past it, and he got his jaws into the brontosaur's long neck.

The tyrannosaur's enormous jaws, activated by muscles as thick as a man's thigh, were so powerful that they could bite through trees. The teeth were splendidly serrated, able to slash, saw, and close on one another like scissors. Complex machines would be designed to their model seventy-odd million years later.

One crunch of these jaws broke the thunder lizard's neck, vertebrae and all.

Pitching forward, tail whipping uselessly, she writhed and heaved in a mighty effort to shake loose. But the fight was ending. The killer forced her down into the mire. Then, without loosening his hold, he chewed until his teeth joined and a great gobbet tore loose from her neck.

Only then did the carnivore back away. Tilting his head upward, he adjusted the mouthful and unhinged his jaws so that the great bloody bundle could slide down into his gullet. For a few minutes he ate, biting hunks and gulping them down. Soon glutted, he stood beside the still-jerking carcass as if pondering what to do. His brain was no bigger than a man's fist.

Giant crocodiles poked their snouts from the lagoon, seeking their share of the meat, but the tyrannosaur trumpeted a warning and they slithered away. The sky darkened as great pterodactyls, the carrion reptiles, swooped in on leathery wings; their wingspreads were wider than those of small airplanes. They too were repelled.

The king of the carnivores took one more massive bite from the corpse. He could not swallow it. The dripping flesh dangled awhile from his yard-wide mouth, then fell into the swamp.

As he shambled away to higher ground, a circle of waiting predators moved in—creatures that flew like huge bats, creatures that coiled or slithered, creatures that strode on four feet or two. All were monstrous.

No human eyes saw this fight. It took place in an unimaginably ancient time, at least a hundred million years before the first tree-climbing, insect-eating shrews (man's first identifiable ancestors) dropped from trees and ventured into open grassland.

We are older than we used to think, but there is no evidence that anthropoids dwelt on earth until long after the giant reptiles had vanished. We know about this particular battle of dinosaurs from fossilized tracks found near the Paluxy River in central Texas—the round tracks of the brontosaur, the clawed prints of the attacker, the thick tail-dragging trails of the scavengers.

Information about their era is sketchy. Throughout recorded history there have been myths in all lands about dragons and other huge, terrible creatures. What inspired these myths?

The first would-be zoologists—Herodotus, Aristotle, and Pliny, for example—wrote down "facts" from hearsay about basilisks, griffins, chimeras, sphinxes, phoenixes, and their ilk, but no real evidence has survived. Nevertheless, in Christianity the dragon is considered the embodiment of evil; the archangel Michael cast out evil from heaven into the earth in the form of a dragon (Revelations 12:9). The patron saint of England, George, supposedly killed a dragon on a hill in Berkshire; even today nothing will grow on that hill.

When the eighteenth century ushered in the "age of rationalism," educated people began to scoff at the notion that dragons and other monsters had ever existed, despite cryptic mentions of them in the Bible. Monsters didn't seem to fit the findings of James Hutton, the founder of historical geology, and others who followed the trail he pioneered.

Hutton, brooding over a Scottish brook that washed sediment down to the sea, glimpsed a dark pit unknown to his contemporaries. He discovered that time is virtually boundless, without beginning or end—as Oriental mystics had always said—but had left its own records in the very stones of the world, in the dust and the clay over which the devout passed to their churches.

Until Hutton, the learned Western world had accepted the biblical version of time, which fixed the universe's age at no more than six or seven thousand years. But natural history, bristling with stubborn facts, wore down this belief. The Bible's accounts of miracles and marvels as well as monsters became entangled in nets of scientific research. Bible stories that don't jibe with known data must be fiction, rationalists said.

By 1791 an English land surveyor named William Smith, digging canals, was pondering the strata of rock exposed by his excavations. He noticed that each layer contained its own characteristic fossils. "Strata Smith," as he came to be called, made the supreme observation that fossils and rocks could be put in chronological order by dovetailing their approximate ages. The study of fossils—paleontology—began.

It is astonishing that fossils exist at all. Living tissue, even bone, decays quickly. It becomes powder and returns to the soil, unless it happens to be buried immediately in some soft material that later becomes rock-hard. Occasionally this does happen; and the earth's long life has allowed it to keep happening. Molds or imprints of billions of organisms great and small are preserved in the ancient rocks that encrust the earth.

Consequently, long ago men began finding strange

shapes embedded in sedimentary rocks such as limestone and sandstone. These discoveries took many forms—impressions of weird plants and fishes, pressed into the solid rock as if into soft clay, and hard stony objects that look like little statues of living organisms.

The ancients invented fantastic explanations for these. But paleontologists read the riddle, and learned where to find many more remains of primeval life forms. From caves, bogs, swamps, stream beds, ice sheets, tar pits, and other places where decay had been prevented, they dug out fossils of creatures that lived millions upon millions of years ago. Footprints, crawl tracks, and sometimes the delicate tracery of feathers and fins were perfectly cast in solid, enduring stone. Occasionally minerals had seeped into the cells of organic matter, transmuting it to rock (petrifying it) without changing its shape.

And so from the abyss of time and from the depths of the earth, the dead came to life. Animals were resurrected from stone, and an astonishing parade of long-dead things marched before man's eyes. But the parade did not include monsters, because the first paleontologists found few monster-size fossils. The age-old talk of such creatures must have arisen from man's own imagination, they decided.

Pieces of fossilized dinosaur bone were dug from Connecticut sandstone in 1820. They caused some curiosity among American scientists, but no one believed that these fossils were valid evidence of monsters. The bone fragments found their way into a drawer of a museum storeroom and were quietly forgotten.

Soon afterward, a few oversized, unclassified teeth and bones came to light in England. Experts admitted, after long debate, that these might be evidence that some bulky creature unknown to science had existed in the dim past. A country doctor named Gideon Mantell, whose hobby was paleontology, kept digging near the site of the discovery, and found more teeth of the same kind.

He took them to London's great museum of natural history, the Hunterian. He and the chief curator went around the collections for hours comparing the teeth with those of every animal, likely or unlikely, to which they might belong. At the end of a discouraging afternoon, Mantell was about to leave when the curator asked, as an afterthought, if he would like to see a model of a strange little lizard from South America, recently mounted for the museum. The two were glumly contemplating it when Mantell bent forward with an exclamation. In the lizard's mouth he saw miniature replicas of the big teeth he still carried in his hand.

The lizard was an iguana. Mantell named his hypothetical monster "iguanodont" (genus *Iguanodon*) to show its kinship. From other fossilized bones in the region, he and other scientists (including the great Thomas Huxley) gradually conjured up an image of a truly awesome reptile between thirty and sixty feet long. It was shaped like a lizard but walked upright, to judge from its thigh bones. It seemed to date back many millions of years, because its remains were found in very old rock strata.

The whole notion of a colossal lizard seemed fantastic—but was confirmed in 1878 when a group of iguanodons emerged from a coal mine in Belgium. They were a thousand feet underground, not in coal but in a fissure filled with marl (muddy limestone). Evidently no less than thirty-one full-grown iguanodonts had tumbled into a deep ravine. It was literally filled for hundreds of feet with the stranded monsters. They had been unable to escape and were entombed in mud as the fissure filled with flood water. The Belgian authorities stopped the coal digging, hewed out thousands of blocks of marl-encapsulated bone, and entrusted a paleontologist named Louis Dollo, still only in his mid-twenties, with reconstructing the skeletons. He devoted the rest of his life to the task. By the turn of the century the Brussels Royal Museum's group display of monsters was a worldwide sensation. The resurrected iguanodonts proved to paleontology that undiscovered apparitions might have been real. A plaque was placed on Dr. Mantell's house: HE DIS-COVERED THE IGUANODONT.

Not only iguanodonts but other enormous unknowns evidently had roamed the land and sea during early tropical ages, long before the first glaciers. In 1868 an unidentified thigh bone as tall as a man was found in the rocks north of Oxford. Excited by the hope of unearthing vast shapes totally new to science, diggers began to pry into all the earth's strata as vast burial grounds of the past.

Some strata did contain evidence of supposedly mythical monsters; museum reconstructions of dinosaurs reminded people of dragons. Beginning in the 1870s, two decades of intense activity exhumed the remains of an astounding assortment of colossal beasts. Sir Richard Owen coined the word *dinosaur,* from the Greek for "terrible reptile" or "terrible lizard."

Meanwhile, geologists were finding their way back through time, studying the record of the rocks through eras measured in hundreds of millions of years. They deduced that the planet had spun hot and lifeless for perhaps a billion years; and then for a billion more it apparently held no life more complex than the speck-size algae in water. Earth reached its afternoon, so to speak, before living creatures first formed the hard shells that make good fossils.

A fossil obviously is as old as the layer of sediment that contains it—younger than those found in the previously formed layers below, older than those in the layers above. Therefore, the fossil record is a vast calendar of the past, with an exciting progression from vanished forms of life to those plants and animals alive on earth today. Layers of sedimentary rock, stacked like so many sheets of paper, are pages in the book of nature.

But the record of the rocks is like a great book that has been abused—its pages are torn, defaced, scattered. The upward push of mountains in birth, advancing and retreating glaciers, sinking of seabeds, earthquakes, volcanic eruptions, and all the dynamic forces of erosion and dispersion have wrecked the once-neat chronological arrangement of the pages, many of which seem to be missing altogether. Nevertheless, the rough outline of earth's story has been reconstructed by careful research that is still incomplete, still going on.

The scientific community divided the vast span of geologic time in which the fossil record seems clear into eras called the Paleozoic (Greek for the time of "ancient animals"), the Mesozoic, or time of "intermediate animals," and Cenozoic, when the "recent animals," the birds and mammals, began contesting for dominant places on land. Manlike fossils appear only in rocks laid down during the last two million years.

If modern methods of geologic dating are correct, the Paleozoic era covered perhaps 350 million years. It was divided into ages, beginning with the Cambrian age (named for an area in Wales where these strata were first uncovered). This was when shelled sea creatures developed their casing and armor and became the most complex life form of their age.

The rise of the monsters began no less than three hundred million years ago—maybe four hundred million—sometime during the Paleozoic era's closing age, the Devonian (from "Devonshire").

They evolved from underwater predecessors—as did all living things. Even now there is no land animal, nor land plant, that does not owe its structure to slow deviations from a water-inhabiting ancestor. There are today certain kinds of lungfish in Africa and Australia that show the evolutionary process by which other creatures worked their way out of the water. During the rainy season these fish swim in rivers, breathing through gills like other fish. But their rivers dry up in summer. Then the lungfish burrow into the mud flats and stop using their gills. They keep alive by gulping air and swallowing it—pressing it down into a bladder that was previously a gas-filled organ enabling the fish to remain buoyant. Now the bladder doubles as a rudimentary lung.

A newt in a pond breathes similarly. These creatures are still in transit—moving ever so slowly across a threshold where countless long-ago forerunners of the higher vertebrated animals made their first gasping ventures into the dreaded atmosphere. "Never make the mistake of thinking life is now adjusted for eternity," the great naturalist Loren Eiseley wrote recently. "There are things still coming ashore. There are other things brewing and growing in the oceanic vat."

In the early Paleozoic era, when the blazing sun rose and set in only a quarter of the time it now takes, when the huge tides of warm shallow seas poured over the rocky lands, when the air stank with gases and howled with gales, forms of underwater life proliferated.

They were almost beyond belief in their abundance, their variety, their grotesqueness, and often their mindless ferocity. There were kite-shaped and cone-shaped carnivores as long as sixteen feet. There were many-legged crawling creatures; wormlike writhing things; blobs and sheets of living jelly; creatures with waving fringes or grasping, sucking tentacles; venomous stinging bottom-dwellers. One species, a tiny sea scorpion, crawled up on the beach and stayed. Others would follow long afterward.

But fish were more mobile and rapacious than other underwater creatures, and became the dominant life form in the Devonian period, which is sometimes called the Age of Fishes. They diversified into at least twenty thousand forms we recognize as kin to modern fish. Many were bigger than man. Some might be called monsters, for they included numerous types of large shark, barracuda, and manta ray—as well as such murderous nonfish as nine-foot water scorpions and two-ton squid that measured sixty-six feet across.

It was in Devonian times, too, that the barren land began to be speckled by plant life. Along shallow shores, the ebb tides left a few sea plants high and dry for part of each day; somehow they learned to adjust to the hard life ashore, learned to use sunlight to perform the miracle of converting salts and minerals into organic matter. In the sea they had been fed and supported, swaying and drifting, by water; on land they needed strong bodies to stay erect. Some met the challenge, spreading over the ground and flourishing in great variety. Gigantic trees grew as high as a hundred feet. Vegetation became luxuriant.

When plants became plentiful on land, this enabled animal life to follow. Within a few million years the land swarmed with spiders, centipedes, worms, crabs, snails. They had to be small to survive. Heavier animals, without strong internal skeletons, would have collapsed under the force of gravity. (In water, of course, buoyancy overcame most of gravity's pull. Even today the most monstrous animals live in the sea.)

Finally, a hundred million years after the first invasion of the land, there came a fateful new penetration of the forbidden element by creatures that could afford to be bulky despite gravity because they had a bracing of bone within.

These were bony, spiny fish. Competition for food in the crowded sea drove some of them into shallows, where they were trapped at low tide, or into swampy lagoons, where the stagnant water lacked enough oxygen to keep them alive. But a few of them refused to die.

Through infinitely slow stages, in asphyxiation and terror, these water failures learned to gulp air through their mouths. To do this they had to push themselves off the bottom, for which their bony pectoral fins were useful. So when a pool dried up completely and they were stranded, they could still breathe, by propping themselves up off the ground and expanding thorax and bladder to suck in air.

By the end of the Devonian era some of these fish found themselves standing on dry land, propped up shakily on four stubby appendages, hobbling in search of new homes. They left footprints across Devonian sandstone. They evolved into those wondrous betwixt-and-between mutants called amphibians, which spent much time on land but always had to return to the water to mate and lay their fragile eggs.

Some of the primitive amphibians had strange

shapes, suggestive of certain hideous creatures imagined by myth makers long afterward. There was something like a monstrous salamander with a head bigger than a crocodile's. There was something that would be called a mesosaur—a spike-toothed, gap-jawed, tail-lashing sea lizard. There were popeyed, grinning things like serpents with horned heads. Some creatures had grotesque raised nostrils and raised eyes so that they could breathe and see while keeping their bodies under water. Some, if they lost a tail or a leg, could grow a new one.

It took a few million years for reptiles to develop from amphibians. One of the most innovative qualities of the reptiles was that their eggs had tough cases and could be deposited anywhere, and their young need not pass through a gill-breathing, water-dwelling stage before crawling onto land. So at last they were freed from bondage to the swamps—and they went on to conquer both lowland and upland. More active than any previous land animals—and more formidable—they filled every niche open to medium-size and large creatures.

Reptiles ushered in the teeming, tumultuous Mesozoic era, during which they were the supreme lords of the earth for roughly 120 million years. Throughout the Mesozoic era, reptiles proliferated in a great variety of shapes, getting bigger and bigger each million years.

Some of them returned to the sea in the form of rapacious swimmers called ichthyosaurs—like giant dolphins but with long, toothed snouts for capturing the slippery fish on which they fed. Some wallowed in swamps, chomping great quantities of plants. Some fed by tearing whole limbs off big trees. Some lurked in dark water, ready to seize other monsters. Some bipeds ran in fifteen-foot strides, as shown by fossilized tracks in coal mined in Wyoming and Colorado.

The enormous reptiles dominated a world of endless forest swamps choked with plants and buzzing with insects. Weather was much the same worldwide, for there were few if any mountains to affect climate.

Almost the entire earth had a tropical or subtropical climate, with fecundity everywhere—the terrible pressure of birth and growth, pressure that squeezed out the egg and burst the pupa, that hungered and lusted and drove creatures relentlessly to kill and feed and copulate. Eventually the crowded forests would be buried in water, over and over again, across huge expanses of the earth's surface. Bedded down in mud, crushed by the enormous weight of sediment piling up above, all this terrifying growth would die and very slowly be compressed into the planet's nearly endless coal beds.

Rooting through fossilized boneyards, paleontologists of our time have identified more than two hundred different kinds of dinosaur. Only the huge bones, a scattering of eggs, and a few colossal tracks are left to impress us with the marvelous organic diversity littering the shores of continents that went down in darkness. The first mammals evolved at about the same time as the first land monsters. But while dinosaurs grew and flourished, the mammals remained tiny and insignificant, probably because they could not compete with the superbly adapted giants.

Until lately, man thought of dinosaurs as cumbersome, dim-witted animals that blundered their way to extinction. "Dinosaur" became the term for anything clumsy, overgrown, ineffective, and obsolete—as though dinosaurs were a laughable example of evolutionary failure, a proof that a small brain in a big body made survival impossible. But science has learned much more about dinosaurs in the past decade.

The picture as it still looked in 1968 was reported by Robert T. Bakker of Yale University:

> Generally, paleontologists have assumed that in the everyday details of life, dinosaurs were merely overgrown alligators or lizards. Crocodilians and lizards spend much time in inactivity, sunning themselves, and compared to modern mammals, most modern reptiles are slow and sluggish. Hence, the usual recon-

struction of a dinosaur as a mountain of scaly flesh
which moved around only slowly and infrequently.

But there was double-think in this view. Man, supposedly well adapted and brainy, has been here only
two million years, most of that time in mean condition,
and is already in danger of extinction if someone
presses the wrong button. Dinosaurs were known to
have ruled the earth, after snatching it from the mammals, for sixty times longer than man has so far. Nobody tried to reconcile their "evolutionary failure" with
their inconceivably long reign.

Another aspect of double-think was that dinosaurs
admittedly had to be devourers and destroyers in order
to find and seize the huge meals they needed—and
were simultaneously assumed to be lazy, cold-blooded
sunbathers like the lizards, crocodiles, and snakes we
know. (A python, for example, needs only one good
meal a year.) Bakker and others began to ask whether
the species might have been misnamed. Maybe dinosaurs were not basically reptilian in some respects.
"Analysis of energy flow indicates," Bakker wrote,
"that dinosaur energy budgets were like those of large
mammals, not elephant-size lizards."

We know that lizards eat little food and have little
energy. They run for only short spurts before flopping
on their bellies to rest in the sun, and cannot remain
on their legs for more than a tenth of their "active"
life. But mammals and birds need and have enormous
energy. A rat burns ten times more fuel for its size
than an alligator; hummingbird muscle uses five hundred times more oxygen than frog muscle of the same
size. Because of their energy, mammals and birds stand
and walk (or run) for almost all their waking life.
Their limbs are under the body to assist them in ambulating. The body of a lizard or an alligator is slung
between its legs.

Most dinosaurs did walk and run, not waddle or
crawl. Their tracks and trails proved this (some fossilized tracks show just the claws of the front feet

touching the ground, like a kangaroo). So did their bones. A solid leg bone means a sluggish creature or one of aquatic habits. Most dinosaurs had hollow bones, indicating that they were active land animals, and disproportionately long hind legs, implying that they walked erect with the short front legs dangling.

Herds of plant-eating monsters, such as three-horned triceratops with immense rhinoceros-shaped bodies, and ankylosaurs, their ambulating tanks studded with sharp spines that must have discouraged any prying, browsed the plains. Sometimes they charged and sometimes they fled when attacked by equally enormous two-footed carnivores like the tyrannosaur or the saber-toothed allosaurus. Certain dinosaurs—for example, the ornithomimid, the ostrich dinosaur—were great two-footed leapers, though they weighed more than elephants.

Other giants not only ran and jumped on hind legs but evolved their forelegs into glider wings (unfeathered) on which they could flap into the air and soar out to sea. Early paleontologists pooh-poohed the possibility of large dinosaur birds because, as Sir Richard Owen said, there seemed no way that "the cold-blooded organization of a reptile should . . . be able to raise a larger mass into the air than could a warm-blooded mammal." Then a specimen with a nine-foot wingspan was found in the chalk of Kent. Rather than retract his assumption about cold-blooded creatures, Owen averred that God was again proving his omnipotence by doing the impossible.

A few decades later the chalk beds of Kansas and Wyoming produced many specimens of a nonesuch that was christened a pterosaur. The wingspans were often twenty-two feet, or about equal to that of a modern light plane. O. C. Marsh, a great American paleontologist, called pterodons "the largest 'flying dragons' yet discovered." There were sound aerodynamic reasons for considering these the largest living things that ever could fly. But in 1972 the first of a spectacular series of finds made scientists drastically revise their theories. In Brewster County, Texas, were found skeletons of three jumbo pterosaurs whose bones indicated wingspans of more than fifty feet. "It is no surprise," wrote Douglas A. Lawson, the discoverer, "that the definitive remains of this creature were found in Texas."

Such startling finds made ever clearer the fact that dinosaurs were not inherently doomed to extinction; they adjusted to their world in marvelous ways and developed qualities needed for long survival. Researchers began to suspect, therefore, that many kinds of dinosaurs were warm-blooded rather than cold-blooded like reptiles.

The test of a good theory is whether it fits together previously unrelated and inexplicable facts. Warm-bloodedness not only explains the stance of the dinosaurs but also helps us understand why they grew so huge. The dinosaurs, unlike furry mammals whose insulation helps them stay warm, lost heat through their leathery skins. But large warm-blooded creatures lose relatively less body heat than small ones. The dinosaur could never have kept its temperature high enough had it been much smaller than it was. This is why no fossils of midget dinosaurs were ever found.

When certain saurians instinctively learned, somewhere in the long Mesozoic era, to generate heat from their own muscles and tissues instead of relying on the sun, as lizards and snakes do, it triggered the rather sudden emergence of dinosaurs from the swamps. Like the fish breathing air, and the amphibian laying shelled eggs out of water, the reptile raising and stabilizing its own internal temperature was a colossal step in the history of life—a major break with heredity.

No sizable mammals could survive around dinosaurs, because the monsters could run down their choice of prey or rear up to pluck it out of trees. For at least a million centuries, and perhaps a third longer than that, dinosaurs dominated the world as completely as men would later. The earth shook to their tread. The waters sprayed and spouted when they dived. All other beasts fled or hid when they approached.

But then something happened to them.

Abruptly, for no clearly discernible reason, in what the encyclopedic science writer Isaac Asimov calls "the most tantalizing problem in paleontology," the dinosaurs disappeared.

3

The Great Dying

"The most hardheaded, blasé geologist is apt to get excited when he becomes involved in a discussion of the extinction of the dinosaurs," said one of the world's leading experts on dinosaurs, Dr. Edwin H. Colbert of the American Museum of Natural History. "The problem is one to which we return time and again, even though very little is known about it."

At first I didn't think the problem was all that peculiar. After all, more than nine-tenths of the world's animal and plant species of past periods are extinct, according to Loren Eiseley. Even though dinosaurs were one of the world's longest-lived orders, why should it be considered so strange that they eventually arrived at the same evolutionary dead end to which most other species came sooner?

Still, I kept finding writers who saw something deeply mysterious in the fact that all these assorted monsters vanished without descendants.

H. G. Wells in his *Outline of History* called it "beyond all question the most striking revolution in the whole history of the earth before the coming of mankind."

Cambridge's noted zoology lecturer Barry Cox wrote, "To a vertebrate paleontologist, this dramatic event is the most fascinating problem of all."

Princeton's vertebrate paleontologist Glenn Jepsen surmised that the problem's solution still lay ahead of us: "The most exciting discoveries about dinosaurs are yet to be made."

As I delved deeper, I began to see what fascinated the experts. Not just one kind of dinosaur but all two hundred kinds dropped out of sight simultaneously. Whether swimmers, crawlers, runners, jumpers, or fliers, they vanished.

The fish-eating pteranodons disappeared from the skies. So did the carrion-eating pterosaurs. So did the rhamphorhynchids, which swooped down on live land dwellers.

The seas seemed to have been abruptly emptied of hadrosaurs with their snorkel beaks, plesiosaurs with their paddlelike legs and elongated necks, ichthyosaurs with their dolphinlike snouts, mosasaurs with their lizardlike bodies, parasaurolophuses with their exotic bony crests swept back like plumes of a cavalier's hat. Whether they fed on fish or aquatic plants, they were gone.

Simultaneously the swamps held not a single plant-eating diplodocus or corythosaur or brontosaur; not one meat-eating megalosaur or deinodont, not one mesosaur with its six-foot crocodile jaws.

The grassy flatlands lost every browsing stegosaur with its armor-plated hide, every towering biped iguanodont, every gentle duck-billed trachodont, every triceratops with its great collar ruff of bone, every barosaurus with its giraffelike neck.

In the trees and thickets not one of the predatory flesh-eating monsters remained. Not the dimetrodont. Not the prosauropod. Not the allosaur. Not the frightful tyrannosaur.

There is not even one survivor that we can see, after a century of searching everywhere for their bones and eggs and tracks. The record of the rocks seems clear.

We know that in rocks from all parts of the world there is a lower layer dating back seventy million years in which dinosaur fossils were found by the thousands. Right up to the top strata of the Mesozoic era, we find all these reptilian species still flourishing unchallenged. There is no sign that they were dwindling in numbers or in health. We can find no traces of enemies or competitors.

Mammals or mammallike reptiles (we're not sure which they were) of the Mesozoic period seem to have been obscure little beasts the size of rats or cats. Probably they still laid eggs and were just beginning to grow their distinctive covering of hair. They lived away from big waters, perhaps in the bleak uplands, as marmots do now. They became fossils so rarely that no complete mammal skeleton has yet turned up in the whole vast record of the Mesozoic rocks.

Then the record is broken. The next rock layer, many feet thick, contains few fossils of any kind. We don't know how long a time this represents. Many pages may be missing here—pages destroyed, perhaps in some worldwide cataclysm.

When next we find abundant traces of the earth's animals and plants, in the Cenozoic era, all the multitude and diversity of the dinosaurs have vanished. Monster reptiles of every kind are gone. For the most part they apparently left no descendants. Only the crocodiles and turtles and tortoises carry on in noteworthy number. Of the giant lizards a few small relatives remain; the largest are the twelve-foot, dragonlike monitor lizards that live only on the island of Komodo in the East Indies.

Instead of dinosaurs, a new kind of life inherited an earth that may have seemed empty. The new layers are crowded with bones of mammal predecessors of the elephant, the camel, the bison, and the horse. The Cenozoic era became the time of mammals. "No trace of a dinosaur bone or tooth has ever been found in any Cenozoic rocks, not even the earliest of them," Dr. Colbert said.

The fossil record reveals many species that gradually died out when a competing group became better adapted. But this wasn't the case with dinosaurs. They had no competitors; their decline wasn't gradual; it was sudden and complete.

Just how long did their annihilation take? Some experts guess five million years, which in geologic time is rapid, but would seem to me a very lingering death for an animal species. Other authorities estimate less than one million years. However, M. N. Bramlette of the Scripps Institute of Oceanography estimates that most Mesozoic sea life disappeared in a few thousand years. Still others think that nearly all kinds of life went into steep decline within a few days. The dead reach of relatively barren rock reduces all the experts to guesswork.

If all the dinosaurs perished in a space of days or weeks, this presumably would have been caused by a catastrophe such as the explosion of a star, showering our galaxy with cosmic radiation of unimaginable strength. "Radiation levels like those following a nuclear war, global storms of extreme intensity, disastrously low temperatures, and the obliteration of the primary elements in the food chain on land and in the sea must have wrought untold havoc. And all this occurring in the space of a week," wrote Adrian J. Desmond, a noted Harvard paleontologist, in summarizing the catastrophe theory.

But Professor Desmond went on to point out that a layer of water can blanket out cosmic radiation—yet the sea monsters as well as the land monsters apparently died, while little tree-dwelling mammals did not. Radiation couldn't have been so selective. He thinks that a sudden worldwide chilling—long enough to make the seas drastically colder, and perhaps to freeze the land at night, but not long enough or cold enough to form glaciers—may have been the event that wiped out dinosaurs. He doesn't speculate much on what might have caused such a temporary chilling.

Whatever happened, it didn't bother certain reptiles. Turtles lived side by side with dinosaurs, and plodded their way right through the Mesozoic and Cenozoic eras, unscathed and unchanged until today. So did a few varieties of lizards. Mesozoic crocodiles have descendants alive now. How did this assortment survive when dinosaurs couldn't?

"The answer," Desmond said, "is at once apparent.

Reptiles are cold-blooded. Dinosaurs were warm-blooded. When the temperature drops, reptiles become cold. Their metabolic rate drops sharply, driving them into torpor and eventually hibernation. But they remain alive, even at ambient temperatures below freezing. It is no surprise, then, that those reptiles which survived were ones that could crawl under logs to hibernate, or, as in the case of turtles and crocodiles, tunnel into river banks for protection. . . . Mammallike reptiles, on the other hand, had insulated their bodies with hair and this feature had been inherited by the mammals. It enabled them to shrink in size yet still survive the exposure. . . . The fact that dinosaurs were uninsulated indicates that they had evolved in climatically equable conditions. If worldwide temperatures dropped, the factor that had spelled success for one hundred and fifty million years would militate against them. As the lizards went into hibernation while the small fur-covered mammals found themselves warm nests, the dinosaurs would have been left out in the cold. Unable to hibernate because of their unwieldy size, these leviathans would have 'frozen' to death."

Plants were blighted too. This seems to support the cold-wave theory. Tropical trees, fruits, and vegetables were evicted by their hardier relatives creeping down from the north. The evergreen conifers, whose spiky leaves help them withstand cold, became widespread. Delicate budding plants virtually disappeared. Since pollen grains are the most durable parts of plants, they are often preserved in the rocks, leaving at least a spotty record of each period's plant life. And this record, wherever early Cenozoic rocks are open to study, shows a time when palmlike plants as well as flowering shrubs were seemingly almost nonexistent. This means that there probably was no food for herbivorous monsters.

Undersea life was thoroughly disrupted at about the time the dinosaurs made their exit. The one-celled plankton in the sea can be traced through the rocks, despite their tiny size, because they are encased in hard shells. Fossils show that plankton that thrived in tropical seas vanished from sediments on those ancient ocean floors. So do fossils of sea creatures that fed on plankton, and those of the armor-plated species dating back to the Devonian age. And so do the far more numerous fossils of ammonites, creatures like squids with coiled shells. These animals occupied only the forepart of their shells; the rest was partitioned into chambers filled with gas that helped buoy them as they prowled for prey on spidery tentacles. All through the rocky record of the Mesozoic period there is a wide variety of these coiled shells. Hundreds of species of ammonites lived, and toward the end of the Mesozoic era they grew more diversified and ornate, producing some exaggerated types as big as six feet across.

When the record resumes, the ammonites are gone. To this day their place has not been taken. No kind of ammonite survives today. The one genus that resembles them, the chambered nautilus, is found only in the warm waters of the Indian and Pacific oceans.

To judge from what we can see today as we peer into that chasm of time, world conditions changed sharply, ending what we call the Mesozoic era. Monstrous reptiles died off fast, together with much—if not most—sea life and plant life. Then later, after a time of trouble for all living things, the environment grew milder again, whereupon mammals developed and spread to fill the vacant world.

But things aren't always what they seem. Biologists, like other scientists, are beginning to understand the treacherous nature of circumstantial evidence.

Even Professor Desmond, the most eloquent expounder of the climate-change theory, has his doubts.

"If cold was responsible for the dinosaurs' annihilation, why did they not persist in the warm equatorial regions?" he asked. "Is it conceivable that the entire globe was subjected to intense cold? It seems unlikely. Even though America and Eurasia were in middle and high latitudes, South America and Africa were more favorably situated climatically."

The same question bothers Dr. Cox. "If the climate did become cooler, one would expect that dinosaurs would have been able to survive in the hotter regions of the world," he wrote.

There are other conjectures.

One is that the earth heated up, rather than cooled, and withered most plant life for a time—which could have starved the herbivorous dinosaurs, and indirectly doomed the carnivorous ones that hunted them. Moreover, sex glands of male reptiles are sensitive to heat; they become sterile when the temperature climbs too high.

Another guess is that the dinosaurs exterminated themselves. Roy Chapman Andrews, the famous naturalist, wrote:

> When the Central Asiatic Expedition, under my leadership, discovered the first dinosaur eggs in the Gobi Desert, we found the skeleton of a small toothless dinosaur right on top of the nest of eggs. There is every reason to believe that it lived by sucking the eggs of other dinosaurs. Possibly it was in the very act of digging up these eggs when it was overwhelmed by a sandstorm. This group of toothless dinosaurs may have become so numerous that they actually exterminated their relatives by eating the eggs as fast as they were laid.

A related theory is that as small furry animals began to evolve in greater numbers, they too raided dinosaur nests for eggs, finally eating them out of existence. Andrews found skeletons of little mammals near where he discovered the eggs. But of course these theories don't account for the simultaneous disappearance of seagoing dinosaurs and other animals and plants.

Some scientists surmise that a global epidemic either wrecked the ecology (perhaps turning many plants poisonous, blighting others, and tainting all the seas, leading to widespread starvation) or directly attacked vast numbers of animals. Perhaps a virulent microbe or virus or insect parasite got a foothold and spread quickly.

A great sickness might not kill all monsters, yet might rob them of their vital drive, and leave them indifferent to problems of survival. Or it might affect the eggs they laid. Today's birds react to stress by laying eggs with thinner shells; dinosaurs might have reacted the same way.

In recent years Bonn University's Institute of Pale-ontology has been studying late Mesozoic dinosaur egg-shells in different strata, and computing trends. Working with thousands of fragments from successive rock lay-ers in the Pyrenees, Bonn has discovered a grim se-quence. Eggs from the older layers are thick-shelled. But in higher (and thus younger) strata, the shells get ever thinner until the last ones are only two-fifths as thick as normal. They must have been pitifully fragile.

The institute found many whole eggs; these obviously had survived the ordeal of being laid but failed to hatch. Perhaps they didn't contain as much calcium as the embryos required. With their hormonal systems hopelessly out of kilter, the dinosaurs would have re-acted by laying weak-shelled eggs, and so sealed the fate of their own young.

In 1973 the Bonn team confirmed its earlier find-ings when it located eight more eggs from the last layer of Mesozoic rocks. Through an electron microscope the eggshells were seen to be so poor that the embryos couldn't possibly have absorbed enough calcium to build complete bodies. The majestic dinosaurs, overlords of the long Mesozoic era, went out not with a bang but a whimper—the whimper of the unborn as they perished entombed in tiny prisons.

At least this is how some dinosaurs went out.

Did all go the same way, even those species that lived under water?

And are they really extinct, every one of the many varieties? Since we can only guess at the kind of fate that overtook them, can we be sure that none survived?

I do know this: deep down in the perpetual night of

the ocean depths, right now and for a long time past, strange things have been happening. I know because I went and looked at evidence, talked with people who had made inexplicable discoveries.

4

Missing and Presumed Nonexistent

"My surprise would have been little greater if I had seen a dinosaur walking down the street," said Professor J. L. B. Smith, a famous fish expert from Rhodes University College in South Africa.

He had seen a fish that couldn't be. A coelacanth.

Since 1858 ichthyologists had been collecting samples of sea-bottom deposits from all the oceans. They had also been studying rock strata on land that was sea bottom in bygone epochs. In 1938, after eighty years of painstaking work, they were certain that no large creatures unknown to them had swum the seas during the last three hundred million years—because satisfactory cross-sections of fossils from all those millennia had been cataloged and classified.

They knew all about coelacanths, they thought.

Coelacanths (pronounced see-la-kanths) were the commonest small fish in the Devonian era, when the only life on earth existed under water. Using their stumpy fins, these fish stirred up the mud of sea floors in search of prey.

But they became "extinct" about the time the dinosaurs did, roughly seventy million years ago. Not one fossil of a coelacanth appeared in any later rocks. And of course no live coelacanths had ever been reported. So there was no chance whatever that the species had hidden out somewhere and continued to exist. Thus spake the experts.

Then came the discovery of December 22, 1938. A fishing boat was trawling off the southern coast of Africa. When it hauled in its nets and dumped the catch on the deck, the three-ton pile of fish included something the crew had never seen before.

It was a fish more than five feet long, weighing as much as a small man, and very much alive, flinging itself about furiously and snapping at anyone within reach. Its bulging blue eyes were so savagely alert that nobody dared to approach too close. It seemed able to breathe air. Not until three hours later did it grow feeble, and finally gasp its last.

It was an unusually ugly fish—rough-hided and heavily scaled, with a powerful jaw and padded fins that stuck out like rudimentary legs. When the trawler returned to port, the manager of the fishing company telephoned the inquisitive curator of the local museum, Ms. Courtenay-Latimer, who often acquired specimens from the trawler captains. She hurried to the waterfront.

She had never seen such a fish before, nor could she find it pictured in any reference book. She made a sketch and sent it to Professor Smith—who unfortunately was on vacation at Knysna, four hundred miles away. The letter didn't reach him for ten days.

Professor Smith, who has discovered and named more than a hundred species of fish, looked at Ms. Courtenay-Latimer's sketch, and felt the tingling excitement of a man on the verge of a sensational discovery. Her sketch showed a coelacanth—a sheer impossibility, since this fish was known only from fossil impressions on rocks laid down millions of years ago. Moreover, the ancient coelacanths were five to eight inches long, not five feet.

We can imagine Professor Smith's dismay when he learned that the fish had been mounted because it had begun to decompose in the heat of the South African summer. But the skin, skull, and part of the spine had been saved. He reassured the curator that she was blameless; she had no way of guessing the immense significance of the specimen, and she had taken full notes of its anatomy before throwing it away. When he got to the museum and confirmed his identification, he showed his appreciation of her work by naming the fish Latimeria.

Newspapers all over the world front-paged the discovery. Someone had netted a specimen of an incredibly ancient group of fish. In fact, it belonged to the group that first crawled out of the sea onto the land. The first amphibians developed from coelacanths, so the coelacanth is a rather direct descendant of our own fishy ancestors. How had it perpetuated itself through the ages, without ever coming to the attention of scientists?

Of course Professor Smith wanted more specimens —fresh-caught ones with internal organs intact. He tried to organize a search expedition, but in September 1939 the outbreak of World War II torpedoed his plans. Nevertheless, he offered a reward of four hundred dollars for another coelacanth, and distributed a descriptive leaflet in English, French, and Portuguese. After the war he and his wife tramped the coast, sailing on fishing boats, distributing the leaflets, and personally impressing on local authorities the importance of the search.

The professor's patience was rewarded after almost fourteen years of waiting. On Christmas Eve 1952 the Smiths got a cable from an English sea captain, Eric Hunt, who ran a trading schooner in the Indian Ocean: HAVE COELACANTH IN COMORO ISLANDS. COME AND FETCH IT.

The Comoro Islands were two thousand miles away, north of Madagascar, and the professor did not have enough money to charter a plane. Knowing that the fish would decay quickly, he appealed to South Africa's prime minister, Dr. Daniel F. Malan, who put a military seaplane at his disposal.

Hoping that Captain Hunt had not made a mistake, Professor Smith flew to the schooner. "To my unspeakable relief," he said later, "the fish turned out to be a true coelacanth. When I knelt down to look at it lying on its bed of cotton wool, I'm not ashamed to say that I wept."

The fish had been caught off Anjouan Island by a

native fisherman, Ahmed Hussein, who had been amazed to pull in a thrashing hundred-pound catch of a kind he had never seen before. Even after being landed, it fought so malevolently that he had to club it again and again. Hussein was unaware of the quest for the coelacanth, and didn't realize that he was damaging the brain of one of the most amazing specimens ever brought up from the sea.

In fact, it was only by luck that this second coelacanth became available for scientific study at all. Hussein hauled it off to market. It was about to be chopped up for food, when a native schoolteacher recognized it as the kind of fish shown in Professor Smith's leaflet. To qualify for the reward, he sent the carcass by bearers twenty-five miles on mountain trails across the island to Captain Hunt, who had given him a leaflet. With great presence of mind, the captain salted the fish and wired for the professor, who arrived just in time to ensure its proper preservation with copious injections of Formalin.

The fish's brain was ruined by the clubbing, and Captain Hunt's crewmen had badly lacerated the body when they incised it for salting. Nevertheless, the body was otherwise well preserved. The skeleton was almost an exact replica—enlarged about ninefold—of primeval coelacanths. Professor Smith would spend the next two years in research on its various parts, including the rudimentary lung-bladder that had kept it alive so long after it was jerked from the sea.

Again the discovery was front-page news. While Smith was still carrying his prize triumphantly homeward in Malan's seaplane, the colonial administrator of the Comoro Islands received a stinging question from his government superiors in Paris: Had he been sunbathing on the beach while foreigners brazenly flew off with France's scientific treasure? Soon afterward Professor Jacques Millot of the Paris Museum of Natural History entered the coelacanth chase. All coelacanths taken in French waters thereafter, he proclaimed, were the property of the Scientific Research Institute of Madagascar. The institute blanketed French dependencies with leaflets duplicating Smith's reward offer, and set up fish-embalming headquarters at strategic ports.

The following September a third coelacanth appeared. Another fisherman, Houmadi Hassani, caught it near the same island where the second had been taken. Leaving his wife to guard the big fish, Hassani ran for Dr. Georges Garrouste, who was in charge of an embalming station. The doctor had often been disturbed by fishermen claiming to have caught "the great old fish," so he questioned Hassani very closely. The fish was large and brown, Hassani said, with white spots and phosphorescent eyes. Dr. Garrouste had seen the previous catch, a steel-blue monster whose popeyes were cold, not luminous. He told the fisherman to go home. A loud argument ensued. Finally the doctor went and looked at the fish. He recognized it as a coelacanth even though it really was brown, white-spotted, with phosphorescent eyes.

By November 1954 the suddenly enterprising French authorities had acquired five virtually undamaged specimens. The fifth and climactic coelacanth, a female, was scooped in alive from 840 feet down. "If we find a female with fertilized eggs," Professor Millot had told officials, "the embryos may reveal life forms receding to unimaginable epochs."

The female was put in a water-filled whaleboat. But after daybreak the sunlight evidently hurt her; she tried to wriggle into the darkest corners of the boat. Professor Millot arrived at noon after a hasty flight from Madagascar. In midafternoon the fish died, belly up. Millot surmised that she died from photophobia, or sensitivity to strong light. He was saddened to find that she carried no fertilized eggs. Nor did a second female, caught in 1960. The hunt went on.

The last time I checked, twenty-eight of these supposedly extinct fish had been caught, ranging in weight from 209 to 43 pounds. Some came from depths of 2,000 feet, all from deeper than 650. Professor Millot and other experts who have studied them say that the angle of their fins varied by as much as 180 degrees between one fish and another, and even sometimes between the two sides of the same fish. (In human terms, this was as if people weren't always born with two forward-pointing feet, but sometimes with two backward-pointing feet, or even with one foot pointing forward and the other backward or sideways.)

This astounding anomaly may shed new light on how fins evolved into arms and legs as fish began spending part of their time ashore. But so far it sheds scant light on how this one species survived the extinction—or disappearance, at least—of so many other forms of life at the time the dinosaurs vanished.

Professor Millot credits the coelacanths' survival to "their great anatomical robustness and the great depth of their habitat." He adds that their reappearance "has been rightly described as 'the most amazing event of the century in the realm of natural history.' "

However, zoologists have been amazed repeatedly by other reappearances.

A supposedly extinct lungfish from the dim past, a neoceratodus, turned up in an Australian river.

A takahe, a nonflying bird like the dodo, was discovered on the South Island of New Zealand.

The king crab or horseshoe crab, unchanged by evolution for at least two hundred and perhaps five hundred million years, has been found from Maine to the Gulf of Mexico, and in Asian waters.

"These stories all prove the same thing," writes Willy Ley at the end of his *Dawn of Zoology*. "Zoology is not yet a static science and the days of discovery are not yet over."

Indeed they aren't. The discoveries include several animals now alive and well (and in some cases here for fifty million years or more) whose fossils have never been seen at all. Until confronted with the actual creatures zoologists were skeptical and amused by natives' descriptions of them. The reports were filed under "mythical and imaginary creatures."

Which is understandable. Scientists must be skeptics. But sometimes they get dogmatic about their skepticism. Many zoologists still blindly follow the lead of Baron Georges Cuvier, Europe's most respected nineteenth-century pioneer of their profession, who chuckled at the idea of unknown survivors from past ages. He declared firmly, "There is little hope of discovering new species of large quadrupeds." But his statement was proved wrong even in his own day.

The shy, solitary tapir had been known to Indians and Chinese for centuries, but Europeans refused to believe that any such creature could exist. When Europeans eventually "discovered" this large oddly colored animal with the droopy nose, Cuvier refused to believe them. He finally got interested when a European shot a tapir and brought back its carcass.

Another "officially nonexistent" monster was part of the folklore of Indians in Argentina. They said that it was as big as an ox, yet could stand on its hind legs, that its front feet were tipped with enormous claws like sickles, and that arrows and bullets couldn't hurt it much. This did sound like something out of mythology, but it proved to be a fairly accurate description of a real monster—the ground sloth, which is a kind of giant armadillo with bony armor plate. Some caves in Patagonia were found to contain bones and skins of twenty-foot sloths weighing as much as elephants. A few zoologists are now willing to admit that giant sloths may still be alive somewhere, although various reports of sightings haven't been officially confirmed.

The duck-billed platypus undoubtedly lives, and has been living for fifty million years, even though savants suspected a "monstrous imposture" when they read the first descriptions of it from a roving biologist, David Collins. He claimed to have seen the creature in New South Wales, and went on to report, "The most extraordinary circumstance observed in its structure was its having, instead of the mouth of an animal, the upper and lower mandibles of a duck."

He did not exhaust the remarkable list of pecularities that distinguish this mixed-up amphibian. He could have added that it lays eggs and then suckles its young by exuding milk from its abdomen; it is equipped not only with webbed feet, enabling it to swim, but also with sharp claws for digging burrows on land, and with poison spurs on its hind ankles for kicking at enemies; it can't see straight ahead, only sideways and upward; it swims under water with its eyes shut, guided by its sensitive bill; in addition to the bill, it possesses horny teeth for crushing the worms it eats; it doesn't mind swallowing large mouthfuls of dirt if its favorite worms are inside.

No wonder zoologists feared a hoax when Collins told them about this nonesuch. Even after the British Museum received a pair of pickled specimens in a cask, some said the things couldn't be genuine. Several decades passed before the museum sent a distinguished scientist, Dr. W. H. Caldwell, to New South Wales to try to find a platypus egg, if any existed. He found two. Eventually the Bronx Zoo in New York obtained two live specimens and kept them in good health for ten years. Scientists don't know why platypus fossils, to say nothing of live specimens, were never found through a century of intensive exploration.

One famous "mythical" creature, the roc, has lately been admitted to museums and textbooks. The roc was best known from the *Arabian Nights* tales of Sinbad the Sailor. It was said to be a giant bird that laid huge eggs. Nobody in the Western world believed in it.

There were hints centuries ago that the roc might be more than imaginary. The great traveler Marco Polo wrote of it as a legend among the Arabs, who gave it its name, *rukh*. He recorded that the Great Khan of Cathay asked for evidence of it. An envoy brought an enormous feather from Madagascar, the island that was thought to be the roc's home. The khan was impressed. Scientists took no notice of Marco Polo's tales.

But the swamps of Madagascar were eventually found to contain bones of a thousand-pound, ten-foot bird that zoologists christened *Aepyornis titan,* or "elephant bird." More impressive than the size of the bird itself was the size of its eggs, which were well preserved in the swamps. They were about three feet around, with the capacity of 6 ostrich eggs or 148 chicken eggs. Roc eggs are still occasionally found on the Madagascan seashore.

But even the Madagascan titans were surpassed by the extinct giant moas of New Zealand. Their scientific name, *Dinornis maximus,* translates as "greatest of the huge birds." They towered twelve feet in height. Probably they were the biggest birds that ever lived—if we don't count the flying dinosaurs, which really were reptiles rather than birds, since they had no feathers. The elephant birds and the moas seem to have been killed off by human hunters about three centuries ago. "Only recently exterminated by man," is the official word on them.

I wondered whether other legendary monsters might have existed too? Superstition has to start somewhere, often with a fact.

As I studied the history of zoological research, I found other weird and fabulous apparitions that must have given rise to exaggerated legends. One was the basilisk.

According to folklore, the very sight of this dreadful reptile was fatal to man and beast: its breath withered vegetation; merely its hissing made serpents flee.

The basilisk is mentioned several times in the Bible's Book of Isaiah (although, depending on the translation, it may be called a cockatrice, another medieval English name for this legendary creature). Shakespeare makes several mentions of the poison of the basilisk, and Shelley in his *Ode to Naples* urged:

> Be thou like the imperial basilisk
> Killing thy foe with unapparent wounds!

The frightful thing was supposedly only two feet in length, but this added to men's fear, because it might approach them unseen. It was thought to have a head with three whitish excrescences that stood upright like a crown, giving the reptile its regal name. *Basilisk* is a Greek word meaning "little king."

A lizard with this type of crown is now well known in Mexico and Central America, and is called the basilisk lizard. It is harmless. But it does have one seemingly supernatural attribute: it can walk on water, and has been photographed doing so. In 1975 scientists analyzed slow-motion films; evidently the basilisk runs atop the water on its hind legs, keeping most of its body off the surface, and retracting each foot with such lightning speed that the feet barely break the surface. So it propels itself somewhat like a high-powered speedboat, skimming along almost entirely out of water because of its momentum.

Another fearsome creature, the griffin, was fabled to be the spawn of a lion and an eagle. A medieval catalog of beasts warns men to stay away from the griffin "because it feeds upon them at any opportunity . . . and is also extremely fond of eating horses." In the Middle Ages, "griffins' claws" were sold in markets. Some of these have survived, and proved to be tusks of extinct mammoths, or horns of the equally extinct woolly rhinoceros, or sometimes horns of antelopes. But the griffin legend goes back at least to Roman times. This half-bird, half-beast was described by Pliny, who didn't believe that it existed. But it was seriously cited by Roman historians as one reason for the mass migration of barbarians who ultimately sacked Rome. They left their native heath, it was recorded, because griffins became too numerous and deadly there.

Fossil hunters have found something like a griffin—at least it was a hybrid bird-reptile, about eagle size. One skeleton, complete except for the head, was found sixty feet underground in a quarry in Bavaria. It was a bird because it was feathered—but it was also a reptile, because of its clawed fingers and long bony tail. An almost identical fossil was found sixteen years later in another Bavarian quarry. This time the head was intact, and contained teeth in its jaws. The relics of these sensational griffinlike monsters can now be seen in the British Museum.

Is the age of zoological discovery now nearing its end? Have all prototypes of imaginary monsters, if they ever existed, been found?

The solid part of the earth's surface has been rather well explored. Certain inaccessible mountain ranges and jungles may yet produce things stranger than we can imagine. But for the rest there isn't much land that man hasn't mapped, photographed, and ransacked for fossils and live specimens. Only the sea retains something of mystery.

What lies hidden in the waters that cover so much of our planet? Mankind has long been frightened and fascinated by this question. If the coelacanth could stay hidden for so long, have other unknown sea creatures done the same?

Consider the kraken.

In Scandinavian folklore the kraken was a gigantic sea monster. Scientists thought it was just another mythological horror. It was first described in 1752 by a bishop named Erik Pontoppidan in his *Natural History of Norway:* "Incontestably the largest sea monster in the world . . . This creature is round, flat, and full of arms or branches."

From this and other details given by Pontoppidan, we can deduce that the kraken is almost certainly what we now know as the giant squid. People knew of squids even in Pontoppidan's day; what they didn't know was how large squids could grow. Even today we're not sure of their maximum size.

We do know that squids have reached out and torn sailors from rafts. They have devoured huge tuna down to the bones before the hooked fish could be boated. They may attack anything—even anchors, boat hooks, or the hull of a ship. Large squids even dare to fasten themselves to sperm whales.

Some people mistake squids for octopuses. This is like mistaking a tiger for a kitten. The biggest octopus has a ten-foot tentacle spread; a squid may be ten times larger. Upper limits are seriously quoted at anywhere from seventy to two hundred feet, although the largest squid actually measured was fifty-seven feet, found on a New Zealand beach in 1888.

The squid, like the octopus, has eight arms with rows of suckers. But the squid also has horny, toothlike rings around the edge of each sucker. And it has two more arms, called tentacles, which can stretch far beyond the reach of the other arms and can retract until almost hidden. These terrible tentacles (sometimes armed at the tip with claws) shoot out to clamp fast on a victim and pull him back into that writhing nest of arms where the parrot beak (twice as large as a man's head) gapes in the center.

We now know from fossils that giant squids (or kraken) have a family history stretching back four hundred million years. Being gill breathers, they have never needed to come to the surface at all. Their deep-sea preferences kept them for centuries in the shadow world, ridiculed by scientists and feared by seamen. Even now the only measurements that biologists can take are from the rare specimens washed ashore. And there's no special reason to believe that the biggest of these deep-sea giants ever do get washed ashore.

At any rate, indirect evidence exists on the skin of captured whales. We know that the suckers of a fifty-foot squid leave circles about four inches across on a sperm whale's skin. And we have found whales with round scars eighteen inches across!

It seemed to me, as I studied the evidence, that other creatures like the coelacanth and the kraken—supposedly extinct or supposedly nonexistent—may live somewhere under the seas. Nature is eternally busy with experiments. Loren Eiseley wrote of popeyed fish seen near the Niger climbing trees with their fins, pursuing worms, and ogling uneasy naturalists who try unsuccessfully to chase them back to the water.

For centuries there have been reports of something lurking in the depths of Loch Ness. However much it might be laughed at, dismissed as something invented by promoters, or explained away as optical illusion, there remained so solid a body of evidence that I felt it was worth investigation.

I decided to begin my own search for modern-day monsters by going to Scotland with my camera crew.

5

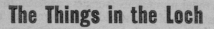

The Things in the Loch

The three fishermen felt their rowboat rise out of the water. The night was dark, and nothing was visible to them on the surface of Loch Ness.

For an instant their boat tilted, almost capsized, but righted itself as it slid back down onto the water. The men, scrambling to stay upright, thought they glimpsed something sleek and dark submerging ahead of them; it seemed about the size and shape of an overturned whaleboat. Presumably this was what had pushed their craft up out of the water.

To this day, the fishermen are sure that they encountered the Loch Ness Monster. They may have been closer to it than anyone else has ever been. But, being close-mouthed Scots and knowing the dour skepticism of their countrymen, they have never reported their experiences to the Loch Ness Phenomena Investigation Bureau, which sifted evidence from 1962 to 1972. What would be the use? They have no real evidence, and not even their own firsthand accounts are valid, for they can't give any precise description of what they saw and felt under them. Moreover, their story is unsubstantiated.

But since 1970 there have been more than a hundred other circumstantial reports—usually with some sort of corroboration—of sightings in the loch or on its shores. In this century the witnesses have included priests, lawyers, gamekeepers, naval officers, and policemen. One eyewitness was a member of Parliament. Another, who commanded a women's auxiliary army-corps unit in Britain during World War II, was the sister-in-law of former Prime Minister Harold Macmillan. Another was a Nobel Prize-winning chemist, Dr. Richard Synge. Still another was a member of the Royal Observer Corps who studied, through binoculars, a big unidentified beast in the loch.

Unlike other mysterious monsters believed to be alive in various parts of the world, whatever lives in Loch Ness is strictly confined. No large creature could get in or out of the loch without being seen. But the loch is far too big for continuous surveillance. Until the end of the last Ice Age, Loch Ness was an arm of the sea. Then the ice on the crags melted, the earth's crust quaked and rose, and the loch was cut off. Wedged between beautiful pine-clad hills that rise more than twenty-two hundred feet, Loch Ness is one of the deepest lakes in Europe, and the largest in the British Isles. Although it is only about a mile wide on the average, it cuts diagonally across Scotland's Great Glen for twenty-four miles, bisecting the Highlands from Fort Augustus on the southwest to Inverness on the northeast. It also serves as a link in the Caledonian Canal, which is the country's main waterway.

Until about 1972 the enlightened world generally regarded the Loch Ness Monster as something conjured up by canny Scots to attract tourists with more money than sense, or as a hallucination seen only by those who partook too liberally of Scotland's most famous product. Yet this monster had a pedigree of sorts, stretching back through fourteen centuries of oral tradition and written reference.

In 565 A.D. the biography of the great Scottish holy man Saint Columba recorded that Columba stood on the lakefront and saw the monster. (Columba was the man who founded Scotland's first Christian monasteries, converting the Picts.) When the creature approached a swimmer who had gone after a drifting boat, he hailed it: "Go thou no further, nor touch the man." The monster went away.

Ever since then, monsters seem to have been appearing in the lake and promptly going away. From a book dating back to the mid-sixteenth century: "No one has yet managed to slay the monster of Loch Ness, lately seen."

About a hundred years later, the memoirs of Patrick Rose (a local laird) mentioned people telling him that a monster was seen in the loch. It was seen again in 1771, according to papers found by Rose's descendant D. Murray Rose.

There is a boys' school at Fort Augustus. An alumnus of that school, Father Francis McElmail, recalled that the monster was "well known to exist" when the school was founded in 1878. The local people had stories of some queer half-seen beast in the loch. They remembered being warned as children not to play on the banks.

But the monster was something of a local secret. Two young brothers named Craig, fishing near Urquhart Castle on a windless day in 1889, saw "a huge form like a sea serpent" heave itself up from the water nearby and wallow off toward Inverness. Affrightened, they rowed ashore. When they babbled their tale to their father, he impressed on them that they must never again speak of what they had seen. Such understandable reticence explains why the monster was little heard of outside the Inverness area.

But with the passing of decades the talk slowly spread. It never died, because reports of sightings became more frequent in this century. One day in December 1903, three men were rowing across an arm of the loch to catch a steamer at Invermoriston when they saw "a hump like an upturned boat" several hundred yards away. As they drew closer it swam off and submerged, as the strange Loch Ness denizens almost always did at the approach of humans.

In 1912 a group of children, hunting birds' nests in scrublands of Inchnacardoch Bay, saw a big animal of uncertain description arise from some bushes and lurch off into the water. They were too horrified to remember exactly what it looked like, but they did agree that it had a long neck and a bulging back. This was almost the first time the monster had been seen ashore; there were recollections of similar sightings in 1879 and 1880 but they weren't disclosed by the eyewitnesses—a group of children in one case, two cousins in the other—until long afterward. Who could say how much credence to give them?

The creature appeared on land again in 1919, according to a Mrs. Peter Cameron, who withheld her story until 1936 (when Loch Ness sightings were becoming more believable). She had been playing on the beach with her two young brothers one Sunday afternoon, when she was fifteen. The children happened to glance across the bay to a marshland shore, where they saw an animal lumbering down toward the water. They imagined it to be a sort of combination camel-elephant: it had a long neck and small head like a camel, but the rest of its body was big and heavy, with broad legs. It "humped its shoulders and twisted its head from side to side" as it went. The children fled home. Their father admonished them to say nothing, and warned that what they had seen was probably something sent by the devil to devour them for desecrating the Sabbath. None of them knew that a similar creature had been sighted seven years earlier on the shore of the very same bay where they had been playing—Inchnacardoch.

"There is no doubt in my mind, and never was, that there was 'something odd' in Loch Ness," a local man wrote in *The Scotsman*. "It was common knowledge; but people did not like being laughed at and you only heard little bits as you got to know the people. . . . After the first war, I had a talk with a priest with whom I had been friends for years, and he frankly said that the story had been going around to his knowledge since before the monastery was built."

It was in 1933 that the Loch Ness mystery first hit front pages. This might never have happened had not a road been built that year around the once-lonely loch, as part of a new Inverness–Glasgow highway.

Dynamite blasted the rocky slopes, pitching boulders and timbers into the dark waters, sending shock waves and echoes rumbling through the glen and the loch. The commotion may have stirred up whatever dwelt

there. Or perhaps the highway itself brought more out-
siders, who talked. And certainly the clearing away of
forest and scrubland gave an almost unobstructed view.

For whatever reason, in 1933 there were no less than
fifty-two separate reports by individuals or groups who
were willing to go on record as having seen something
big and unidentifiable in the loch.

Many of these accounts merely spoke of a mysterious
commotion in the water, or a great boiling without visible cause. A wake like that of a motorboat might sweep
across the surface—a narrow, widening track of heaving waves and froth—when no boat was in sight.

But there were several dozen people at various times
who thought they saw a long hump "like an overturned
boat," as many described it. Some watched it from afar
for as long as ten minutes, while it slid along through
the water at good speed or rolled and plunged before
submerging. In one case two people at different points
along the shore independently reported seeing a six-foot
hump moving fast on the surface at approximately the
same time, 11:45 A.M.

The publicity was slow in gathering momentum. By
June 1933 a Glasgow paper, the *Daily Express*, was
publishing intermittent cautious notes such as these:

[June 9] A monster fish which for years has been
somewhat of a mystery in Loch Ness was reported to
have been seen yesterday at Fort Augustus.

[June 28] Two men and two women who were
boating on Loch Ness had an unpleasant and exciting
experience today. The "monster" rose out of the water
about fifty yards from the boat. One of the women
fainted.

[August 12] An effort to photograph the Loch Ness
Monster is to be made by Captain Ellisford, a well-
known amateur photographer. He arrived in Inverness
today with a large box of modern photographic material. He will use a telephoto lens.

However, the local tourist board's annual report, published September 13, made no reference to any ap-

paritions in the loch. Local people were still unwilling
to talk to oustiders about such phenomena.

The excitement really began in October, when news
got out about an incident on September 22. Three
Canadians—the Reverend W. E. Hobbes, his wife, and
his sister-in-law—walked into a lonely tearoom on the
lakefront near Altsaigh, only to find the room deserted.
They called out. A voice upstairs replied, "We can't
come down yet. We're looking at the Monster."

The visitors hastened up the stairs. There, two ladies,
named Fraser and Howden, stood on a balcony, watching a moving object in the loch about a thousand yards
away. They could make out a snakelike head and neck,
turning from side to side, ahead of two low humps and
a tail of indefinite length splashing the surface. After
about ten minutes it submerged.

It had been too far away to estimate its size. But to
be visible at that distance, its dimensions must have
been considerable. The Reverend Hobbes wrote: "My
wife and her sister were naturally excited at beholding
this marvellous sight, but the proprietress of the tea-
shop [Miss Janet Fraser] took the matter quite calmly,
remarking that she had seen the 'Monster' three times
before."

Upon learning of this, *The Scotsman* rushed its own
correspondent to Loch Ness, recalling him from a trip
aboard a destroyer. He reported that the summons
caused "more merriment than serious interest" in the
ship's wardroom. Nevertheless, he journeyed to the
loch and interviewed many people who claimed to have
seen something frightening there. "It didn't take me
long to decide that, with one or two probable excep-
tions, the witnesses were telling the truth," he wrote.

After his first long article appeared, London newspapers sent reporters north. The October 23 *Daily Express* gave a whole page to the mysterious monster.
London radio stations began broadcasting bulletins
from Loch Ness.

Letters poured in to Scotland's Fishery Board sug-
gesting ways to catch the creature. Special trains were

run from Glasgow and Inverness to the loch to convey
the curious. A passenger steamer began making sight-
seeing cruises thrice daily. Its captain, Duncan Cameron, told a reporter, "Everyone comes aboard claiming
total disinterest in mythical monsters. Then for three
and a half hours their eyes never leave the water."
Captain Cameron himself eventually admitted having
seen "some slick gray object with a hump shape" in
Loch Ness three times in eighteen years.

As I delved back through news accounts of the
carnival of monster seekers in 1933, I wondered whether E. G. Boulenger, director of the aquarium at the
London Zoo, might have been partly right when he
wrote that the Loch Ness Monster was "worthy of consideration if only because it presents a striking example
of mass hallucination. . . . [We] should find no difficulty
in understanding how the animal, once being said to
have been seen by a few persons, should have shortly
after revealed itself to many more."

Autosuggestion—a preconceived idea planted by the
desire to see something—may indeed have been at work
among hundreds of people who reported strange sights
at the loch since 1933. But the photographs taken by
Hugh Gray and Dr. Kenneth Wilson were not imagin-
ings.

On Sunday, November 12, 1933, Gray took his usual
after-church walk near his house on the shore at Foyers.
The path led along a cliff about thirty feet high. Suddenly he saw the calm water below him heave up, and a
rounded back and tail burst into sight.

Nothing he could identify as a head appeared. He was
carrying his camera, as was usual on his walks, and
managed to snap five pictures during the few moments
the animal thrashed on the surface. Because of the spray
it was throwing up, Gray didn't think his snapshots
would show much. He was a long-time employee of an
aluminum works at Foyers, and he said later, "I was
afraid of the chaff which the workmen and others would
shower upon me." So he left the film in a drawer. He
knew that hoaxes had been attempted in other years.
Once a dark object on the loch turned out to be a string

of barrels with a make-believe animal's head attached. Another time, tracks imputed to a monster were found to have been made by pranksters with a stuffed hippopotamus foot.

Weeks later, Gray's brother took the film to Inverness to be developed. Only one of the five shots came out. It showed a long writhing body, shrouded in spray, as Gray had described to his brother. Kodak technicians examined the negative and certified that it hadn't been doctored. Newspapers published the photo; zoologists at first could think of nothing to say.

Professor Graham Kerr of Glasgow University called the picture "unconvincing." J. R. Norman of the British Museum of Natural History said, "It does not appear to me to be the picture of any living thing. My personal opinion is that it shows a rotting tree-trunk which rises to the loch surface when gas has generated in its cells." W. T. Calman, also of the British Museum, said he wouldn't believe in any monster until he examined a specimen. Scientists, he claimed, deal only with specimens. This wasn't strictly true, for zoological catalogs list several kinds of whales that have only been sighted, not caught.

Of all the evidence that has accumulated in the past forty-three years, one photograph has been the most widely published. It became known simply as the Surgeon's Photograph, and may still be the only clear shot of the head and neck of the Loch Ness Monster.

The man who took the series of snapshots including this famous photo was Dr. Robert Kenneth Wilson, a quiet, thin-faced gynecologist who was to later serve as an artillery colonel in World War II. His reputation for integrity was well known in London's Harley Street, where he practiced, and was vouched for by Eric Parker, editor of the noted British natural history magazine *The Field*.

For professional reasons Dr. Wilson soon shunned all connection with the famous photograph. He eventually left England with his family and settled in Australia, where he died in 1969. Because of his distaste for publicity, the circumstances of the picture taking were never quite clear. But by piecing together letters from him and his widow, and contemporary press accounts, we can reconstruct the situation.

He had leased some land near Inverness for bird shooting. In the early spring of 1934, he and an unnamed friend decided to drive north to visit the place and take photographs of wild fowl. Accordingly, he borrowed a quarter-plate camera with a telephoto lens. After driving all night, he stopped about seven-thirty along the new road three miles beyond Invermoriston, at a point where the road is two hundred feet above Loch Ness. Dr. Wilson continued in a letter:

> I noticed a considerable commotion on the surface some distance out from the shore, perhaps two or three hundred yards out. I watched it for perhaps a minute or so and saw something break the surface. My friend shouted, "My god, it's the Monster!"
>
> I got the camera and then went down and along the speed bank for about fifty yards to where my friend was, and got the camera focused on something which was moving through the water. I could not say what this object was as I was far too busy managing the camera in my amateurish way.

Dr. Wilson took four photographs in about two minutes, before the animal dived and disappeared. The date was April 1—April Fool's Day, as he soon realized. Wondering whether he could have been fooled, or might be accused of attempting foolery, he drove on to Inverness and got the plates developed.

Two were blank failures. The third showed the small head and long graceful neck arched over the water, now so familiar from eyewitness accounts. The last plate showed a smaller object—apparently the head about to submerge.

On advice of the chemist who developed the pictures, Dr. Wilson sold the best photograph to the London *Daily Mail*, which published it on April 21. But he wouldn't tell the editors anything more than the basic facts, and wouldn't try to estimate the creature's size. He never claimed that it was "the Monster." He had simply photographed "an object moving in the waters of Loch Ness," he said. "I am not able to describe what I saw." With that he withdrew forever from the wrangling that inevitably follows any photographs purporting to show a live monster.

As in the case of Hugh Gray's photo, the scientific world resolutely closed its eyes to what might be one of natural history's most sensational discoveries. Dr. Calman again refused to guess what these new photos showed, reiterating his indifference to anything less than an actual specimen. Others called the object a tree, or the tip of a diving otter's tail, or the body of a grebe or cormorant or some other bird in the act of diving into the water.

By implication they disbelieved the London physician's statement that there was "an object moving in the waters," and ignored the evidence of his second photo, which was hazy but showed a head that was clearly similar to the first. Its proportions were the same although the scale and angle were different. Obviously Dr. Wilson couldn't have changed plates in time to get two shots of a diving bird or otter.

In New York, Dr. Roy Chapman Andrews of the American Museum of Natural History offered a slightly more adroit explanation:

The picture showed just what I expected—the dorsal fin of a killer whale. A killer's dorsal is six feet high and curved. It would make a wonderful neck for a sea-serpent. Doubtless the whale had made its way through the narrow gate of the loch from the open sea.

Doubtless.

One of the most impressive eyewitnesses seemed to be Alex Campbell, a fisheries official at the loch. He saw a monster for the first time on a calm May morning in 1934. He was standing on a spit of land lear Fort Augustus when suddenly "a strange object seemed to shoot out of the water almost opposite the Abbey boathouse. The head and neck stood about six feet out of the water. The neck was about one foot thick, curved and tapering like a swan's. The head was the size of a cow's, but flatter, with a serpentine look about it. Then there was a humped darkish body stretching about thirty feet behind, I reckon. The thing seemed to be nervous, twitching its head from side to side." The probable cause of its nervousness soon hove into view: two herring trawlers at the mouth of the Caledonian Canal. At sight of them, the animal ducked under water and disappeared in a boiling swirl.

During seventy-four years spent around Loch Ness, including forty-seven years as one of its water bailiffs, Campbell has seen strange things in the water eighteen times. Once he saw two creatures near Borlum Bay— one large dark hump moving away from him, churning the surface, while another hump lazed almost motionless near Saint Benedict's abbey.

Serious students of the Loch Ness mystery don't claim to be seeking an ageless specimen confronted by Saint Columba centuries ago. They think of the loch as home for a small but viable species of monsters— not necessarily all identical. Some might have humps, others not. Some might have small horns as snails do (an occasional witness has reported seeing horns), while others might have a flat serpentine head. In eighty or a hundred million years of evolution, who knows what divergent lines might have developed?

After the first sensational sightings, there were no further important revelations about the loch's denizens for a long time. So in 1934 the press lost interest. No scientist dared to say that he considered the Loch Ness reports and pictures worth investigating. The view of the establishment seemed to be summed up in a scorching statement by Mr. Boulenger of the London Zoo, who had previously attributed all the sighting to mass hallucination: "The whole business is a stunt foisted on a credulous public and only excused by a certain element of low comedy."

Although the world forgot Loch Ness, the creature or creatures kept appearing and disappearing, and Scottish papers often carried reports as mere matters of fact.

The Glasgow *Herald* published news of sightings fifty-one times between 1934 and 1956. Occasionally one of these was picked up by some London paper, but Londoners merely chuckled.

After a hiatus in widespread monster watching for almost a quarter century, interest began to pick up again in the late 1950s. Mrs. Constance Whyte, having spent eight years collecting accounts from people living near the loch, published her book *More Than a Legend* in 1957.

An educated woman with an interest in Scottish history, she was the wife of the manager of the Caledonian Canal, so she knew a lot about Loch Ness. She herself never saw any monsters, despite living thereabouts for twenty-three years—but, she wrote, "a book had to be written. Friends of mine had been subjected to ridicule and contempt, and I felt it was time to counteract the flippant and frivolous attitude of the media."

Her book contained several photographs taken in the 1950s. One seemed to show three humps in a line; their contours made it unlikely that all were part of the same animal. Another picture showed what might be a hump, and, slightly ahead of it, a smaller protuberance that might be a half-submerged head. If the two were connected, measurements indicated that this monster could be fifty feet long.

By piling up masses of consistent evidence, Mrs. Whyte moved a few technical researchers to investigate. Dr. Denys W. Tucker, a zoology lecturer at Oxford University and a scientific officer at the British Museum, told his students that the Loch Ness phenomena were worth probing. Thirty students from Oxford and Cambridge planned a month-long expedition during summer vacation—whereupon the British Museum dismissed Dr. Tucker from the post he had held for eleven years. The students took to the field with cameras and an echo sounder, but they got little except one brief sighting of a ten-foot hump and some unusual echo traces.

Meanwhile, a monster buff named Timothy K. Dinsdale, an aeronautical engineer, took a statistical approach. He broke down the details of hundreds of sightings, and put together a picture of the monster or monsters as reported by the preponderance of evidence: small head, long neck, large body with varying humps, four flippers, and short rounded tail. Wording that recurred in many reports made astonishing reading:

"Humps churning through the water leaving a foaming trail. . . . Head about the same width as neck, mouth twelve to eighteen inches wide. . . . Looked like an elephant's back, twelve feet long. . . . Wake like from a torpedo. . . . Speed at least ten miles an hour."

Pondering the composite description, Dinsdale and Tucker and Mrs. Whyte all thought they saw the dim outline of a fantastic possibility—the ghost of a great dinosaur.

If you glance back to the chapter on dinosaurs you'll notice the giant aquatic reptiles called plesiosaurs. To judge from skeletal remains of plesiosaurs in both salt- and fresh-water deposits around Great Britain, they were very much like the description of today's denizens of Loch Ness.

Adapted for life in the open sea, plesiosaurs grew to thirty feet long. They had a barrel-shaped body with a hefty tail, four paddlelike limbs, a long slender neck, and a tiny head with a large mouth and pointed teeth. They ate fish, of course—which meant that they probably had to be fast swimmers to catch their prey. And they sometimes lurched onto land.

Until 1952, when the second coelacanth was caught, few scientists could accept the notion that any species could still be alive after seventy-five million years of apparent extinction. But the rediscovered coelacanth was "a stern warning to scientists not to be too dogmatic," as Professor J. L. B. Smith wrote at the time. The warning was renewed when specimens of the genus *Neopilina,* a small mollusk believed to have been extinct for three hundred million years, turned up alive in 1957. So there were precedents for the theory that the supposedly extinct plesiosaurs might have lived on, perhaps in evolving forms, in the dark depths of Loch Ness.

In the face of scorn and ridicule, investigators at Loch Ness have managed to compile what I consider the fullest evidence for the existence of any monster anywhere on earth. The famous British author G. K. Chesterton once wrote, "Many a man has been hanged on less evidence than there is for the Loch Ness Monster." Nevertheless, proponents of any theory about a monster need more than an endless accumulation of sighting reports to convince the scientific world. Knowing this, Dinsdale went to Loch Ness in 1960 hoping to film the monster with a borrowed 16mm movie camera. For five days he rose at dawn and patrolled various sectors of the shore, binoculars and camera at the ready, without sighting anything.

By chance on his last day, April 23, he did get a few feet of film. He was driving slowly along a cliffside road three hundred feet above the glassy black water when he spotted "a long oval shape, a distinct mahogany color," floating about three-fourths of a mile away. "It had fullness and girth and stood well above the water," he wrote in his book *Loch Ness Monster*. "Abruptly, it began to move. I saw ripples break away from the further end and I knew at once I was looking at the extraordinary humped back of some huge living creature."

As he snatched his camera and began shooting, the creature swam in a slow zigzag, then turned and submerged, throwing up a tremendous wash of foam. At first Dinsdale tried to keep his film a secret, hoping to show it privately to scientists. But word leaked from the film laboratory. In June his footage of the swimming monster was shown on BBC television, and later on TV programs all over the world.

To the untrained observer it showed little—just a sizable blob moving through the water. Again zoologists scoffed. Some said it showed men rowing a fifteen-foot boat, "no uncommon sight on Loch Ness." Others claimed it was a heavy-laden motorboat belonging to a Foyers man named Jack Forbes; by producing a personal name, these attackers made their "exposé" seem devastating.

Nevertheless, their hypothetical boats bore no relation to the size and shape of the moving object in the film. Foreseeing just such attacks, Dinsdale had purposely filmed a motorboat following the same course as the monster. Even to the naked eye, the objects were very different, and the boat could clearly be seen for what it was. This made no difference to zoologists. They would not be moved by something that cut across the natural order of things. Officialdom remained cool to proposals for financing a scientific investigation.

So it remained for a small group of amateur naturalists to set up the Loch Ness Phenomena Investigation Bureau. Among them were Sir Peter Scott, son of the great Antarctic explorer; Richard Fitter, ornithologist from the London Zoo and nature correspondent of the *Observer;* Mrs. Whyte; and Highland laird David James, a former member of Parliament and wartime torpedo-boat skipper.

They registered the LNPIB as a charity, with any profits from its work to go to the World Wildlife Fund. "We claim no proprietary rights," James announced. "If any individual or group wishes to pursue independent research, all information available to us is at their disposal." The Chicago Adventurers' Club put up five thousand dollars to get the bureau started. Dinsdale gave up his aeronautical job and committed himself wholly to the search for whatever dwelt in the loch.

In 1964 the bureau persuaded photographic-interpretation experts in the Royal Air Force to examine the Dinsdale film by twentyfold optical enlargement, frame by frame. The resulting report was a two-thousand-word document in guarded military phraseology.

It said that the object rose three feet from the waterline, moved at about eleven miles per hour, and was definitely not a surface craft or submarine, "which leaves the conclusion that it is probably an animate object." As for its size, the RAF speculated that it might be thirty or forty feet long and "not less than six feet wide and five feet high."

Suddenly the laughed-at Loch Ness Monster was almost considered respectable. Many scientists still ridiculed it, but raising money became easier, and more scientists joined the hunt, including Roy P. Mackal, University of Chicago biochemist, who was to make it his major hobby for ten years.

The bureau's first goal was to get photographs that were convincing enough to jolt moneyed organizations into backing a more ambitious search with electronic detecting and tracking equipment. To send divers down would be futile, because a suspension of peat carried down by mountain streams made the water so murky that light penetrated only a few feet. The bed of the lake had been tested; its almost flat bottom (eight hundred feet down) was composed of a three-foot layer of surprisingly fluid sedimentary mud.

Hoping for good photos from shore, the bureau mounted a watch each summer. A crew of eager volunteers, recruited from England and America, for a week or two at a time, armed themselves with cameras and binoculars and drove specially equipped vans to vantage points. On good days they could observe virtually the whole surface of Loch Ness.

The field director of this expedition was Clem Skelton, a monk turned free-lance film director and intense believer in the Loch Ness monsters. During the long frigid Highland winters, when there was little daylight and the tourists abandoned the shores, Skelton and his wife stayed in their trailer near the water. Their closest neighbor may have been a monster.

Six times Skelton saw what he thought was a monster. Once, he said, he was practically on top of it. "I was rowing a boat. I looked over my shoulder and there it was. It was the classic upturned-boat sighting, surrounded by boiling foam, but it was bigger than my boat and if anyone wanted to win at Henley he should have rowed as fast as I did to get out of its way."

The bureau got several movie shots of a purported monster, all at long range. One apparently showed the humps of two big creatures moving side by side through the water. Another showed something big but indistinct, in motion on a small pebbly beach. The trouble with these films, as with the Dinsdale film, was that they were unspectacular. Nothing in them was clearly monstrous.

In 1966 the bureau logged thirty-two sightings by expedition members and others. Encouraged by these reports, Field Educational Enterprises of Chicago gave twenty thousand dollars to buy better long-range cameras. But the summer of 1967 passed with only nineteen sightings, none dramatic.

Public interest waned again, but it got a new lift in 1968, when scientists from the University of Birmingham, England, brought in a new type of sonar apparatus and picked up underwater echoes that seemed suggestive. There were sounds from "a large object," dubbed Object A, which dived and rose, moving in and out of the sonar beam, for about ten minutes. During this time it was joined by Object B (almost certainly a school of fish, from its echo characteristics) and Object C—which behaved remarkably. C moved at fifteen knots and dived at a velocity of 450 feet per minute.

The report, by Dr. Hugh Braithwaite, who headed the expedition, continued: "Since Objects A and C are clearly comprised of animals, is it possible they could be fish? The high rate of ascent and descent makes this seem very unlikely, and fishery biologists we have consulted cannot suggest what fish they might be."

As usual, scientists scoffed. The Birmingham equipment, they said, must have registered a false image, as sonar sometimes does. It had picked up a "ghost," not a monster. The Birmingham team made more sweeps of the loch in 1969 and 1970, but didn't risk further scorn from colleagues: it kept its findings secret.

Some U.S. sonar experts joined the hunt in a chartered motor vessel, chugging up and down the loch at all hours of the day and night, sending "pings" from a specially adapted Honeywell sonar. They made some strange contacts. Once they tracked what seemed to be a large animal for more than two minutes. Another time they detected two large objects passing through the beam; a few minutes later one of the objects passed back in the opposite direction, showing the reverse shape.

From 1968 on, expeditions frequently succeeded in tracking large underwater objects on sonar. Usually, to gain scientific acceptance, researchers need only demonstrate that they can repeat a result under controlled conditions. This has been done again and again in the past decade at Loch Ness. Some scientists, however, still won't look at the results.

At any rate, one wealthy Bostonian did look at the results, and he got excited. This was Robert R. Rines, a successful patent lawyer and inventor (and former Harvard faculty member) who had dabbled in science ever since he and a few friends founded an organization called the Academy of Applied Sciences in 1963. The institution, which has no connection with any university or permanent research organization, stays discreetly vague about its membership and aims. In 1971, Rines and his academy team brought an underwater electronic stroboscopic camera to Loch Ness.

They used it for two weeks in August, but reported no sightings. In 1972, however, they got four pictures in quick succession, showing a large mass with what some experts identified as a flipperlike appendage. At the same moment, the sonar beam—which was aligned with the underwater camera—registered something huge very near the camera.

And so it came to pass that after being sought for forty years, one of the strange, elusive giants finally exposed itself to close-up photography. The sonar readings cross-checked with and authenticated the photos. Here at last was indisputable proof of the presence of some enormous creature.

The photos and sonar chart were studied in secret by leading authorities on sonar, photograph interpretation, and marine zoology. Even the British Museum had to take notice. Its experts examined the material in October, and unbent enough to make a statement: they were convinced that the photos were genuine and that a large, unidentifiable moving object was shown.

Zoologists in the U.S. were more explicit. Members of the Smithsonian Institution declared that the creature in the photos "has the shape of the tail of the palmate newt." (A newt is a tailed amphibian rather like a lizard.) Authorities at the New England Aquarium said, "It does not appear mammalian. The general shape and form of the flipper does not fit anything known today."

Sonar wizards estimated that the animal was twenty to thirty feet long. Photographic experts decided that the flipper was six to eight feet long and two to four feet wide. The taillike structure visible in the fourth picture was reckoned "at least eight feet long."

These findings broke the solid front of the scientific world. Several fairly well-financed teams of scientists paid extended summer visits to Loch Ness. The National Geographic Society, the *New York Times,* the National Broadcasting Company, and a Japanese technical group have sent crews in recent years. The Rines group has been there every summer. In 1975 Rines's cameras took thousands more flashlighted photos deep in the murky water, and got two more photographic "equivalents of a Rorschach test," as one still-skeptical news magazine called it. "Depending on the eye of the beholder, one showed what could be a large body with a long neck, the other what might . . . be a hideous, horned head."

I decided it was time to take a look for myself. In July 1976 my camera crew and I went to Loch Ness.

As we flew over Scotland's jagged west coast we could see how the shore had been torn to ribbons by the sea in ages immemorial; bays and inlets had eroded away, and mountains were worn down. The air view showed us that Loch Ness lay along a geological fault line, a string of deep narrow lakes slashing across Scotland from the Firth of Lorn on the west coast to Moray Firth on the east coast. That whole diagonal must have been an ocean channel millions of years ago.

Driving up into the Highlands, I discovered how awesome they are. We crossed great uninhabited tracts of moorland as blasted and witch-haunted as anything in *Macbeth;* we wound through passes where the dark, hard, sorrowful hills rose up against the skyline, imprisoning bare and brown little valleys.

The Highlands have always been hungry lands, often too hard and bitter for plow or pasture. The millennia have scarcely turned the sod or stained a stone. We saw outcrops of the oldest rock in the world, the earth's original crust. As we climbed, the human world began to dwindle. Our crew fell silent amid the great terrible loneliness. It was just as well that the road was good, I thought, for it was about the last thing to look at. Towns were few and far apart. Trees were sparser and less tidy. The mountains hung beautifully aloof, seeming unconnected to the earth, set apart in a shimmer of changing clouds and colors and skies.

Late that afternoon we drove down along the south shore of Loch Ness. We took the old narrow road built by General Wade after the Jacobite rising of 1715. My first impression of this ancient lake was one of size and grandeur: great dark mountains rising steeply from the mirrorlike waters, beneath a huge epic sunset. I was surprised at how little I could see from Wade's road, because of the bushes and birches and pines lining the shore. Since this was the only road until 1933, I could understand why travelers almost never noticed anything in the loch.

Skirted by new roads and the site of an aluminum plant, from a distance the loch might seem part of a cheerful, bustling modern world. But at close range it seems quite different. The strange Celtic aura of timelessness lingers around the silent water.

Little has changed since Scotland's first two intrepid tourists, Dr. Johnson and Mr. Boswell, rode rather breathlessly down the road to Loch Ness on a pair of overburdened ponies. Johnson was disturbed by the wildness of the scene, the rocks "towering in horrid nakedness" above the loch. I could understand how he felt.

Perhaps because of the legends of its monsters, the place strikes some visitors as peculiar. The nature writer Gavin Maxwell thought the loch "seems to reach out at you as if it were a thing sentient and aware, creating a feeling of unease even under a summer sun." Percy Cater, one of the first English journalists to go there in 1933, wrote after a second visit in 1955:

> The Loch oppresses me as much as it did when I first saw it twenty years ago. It remains as enigmatic as the face of Mona Lisa. . . . Its surface, suggestive of its sinister depths, is as forbidding as anything I know. . . . In this harsh landscape it is easy to think of strange goings-on.

The summer nights are not really dark; instead, there is a perpetual moonstruck twilight. The half light seems not restful but foreboding—especially if you know something of local history. Surprisingly strong currents can catch the unwary boater on Loch Ness, and more than one has rowed or sailed onto the loch and never been seen again. Due to its great depth, the bodies of drowned people are rarely recovered.

The dangers of the loch have kept the monster legends free from hoaxes in which pranksters float a simulated monster in the water. The model would have to be propelled somehow, presumably by someone under water, and then it would have to be pulled under before anyone had time to discover what it really was. But nobody wants to go swimming in Loch Ness. Even rubber-suited divers dislike going into it, because of the underwater darkness and the steepness of its banks.

With all the publicity the monsters have stirred up in the past decade, I thought tourists armed with binoculars and cameras might line the shores, and rowboats might be as thick as in MacArthur Park. But even in July, near the peak of the tourist season—and in a week when a heat wave in the British Isles had pushed temperatures up into the seventies, sending many Lowlanders in search of coolness in the glens and lochs—Loch Ness was pleasantly uncrowded.

There are a few good places to sit and watch the water, but the weather turns cold and windy so often that few monster seekers will stand vigil regularly. Boats are surprisingly rare on the loch. Fortunately, I'd made arrangements for one.

Far more surprisingly, our camera crew had beginner's luck.

The morning of our first day out, July 4, the sky was clear and bright, and the loch's surface was flat and calm. I was gazing down into the opaque depths, musing that down there was my past life and the lives of all my ancestors back to the first blob of jelly in the first primeval sea—when someone nudged me and pointed.

Out on the still water, a V-shaped wake had emerged. Our cameras were pointed at it, and running.

Many people who have seen what they think was the Loch Ness Monster have mentioned the big wave or wash the creature generated. Now I could understand. It was startling to see the broad path of jumping water spread and lengthen behind some invisible moving object beneath the surface, as if a small submarine were gliding along just under the water.

It moved rather fast—perhaps ten miles per hour— at a considerable distance from us. Within a minute it had churned out of range of our cameras. No one was in sight on the lake or ashore, so we may have been the only eyewitnesses to this particular appearance.

Whether it was giant eel or sea slug, plesiosaur or vastly enlarged newt, or something totally new to us, we recorded unmistakably on film the big wake it threw up as it plowed along beneath the surface. Perhaps you've seen this, or will see it, on my television shows.

But it will remain a mystery for a while longer. No one yet has obtained the definitive picture. Success depends largely on luck. Until a living specimen is captured for scientific study, we can only guess what kind of monstrous things have been living for so long in Loch Ness.

6

Dark Worlds Below

Deep water is an environment more hostile to man and his endeavors than is outer space.

An astronaut can see what is around him, can readily communicate with his fellow beings, and can sometimes work in shirtsleeve comfort. But not the deep diver.

Under water, sunlight and radio waves penetrate only feebly below one hundred feet, and hardly at all below two hundred. Near the bottom, the waters are usually murky with mud or clouds of organisms, so even with lights the visibility is often limited to about a foot. Deep divers can't be well protected against the penetrating chill, which saps their vitality and slowly fuddles their senses.

Consequently, on the rare occasions when a man steps out of a protective capsule a few hundred feet under the surface, he feels none of the space-walking astronaut's exhilaration and sense of freedom. Instead, he is nearly blind, very cold, very lonely, and aware that if he loses his way in the dark he cannot get back to the surface on his own.

Even from within the best submersible spheres yet built, underwater exploration is still a difficult and largely unknown frontier. Ten years ago we thought the day of the aquanaut was at hand: the U.S. Navy's Sealab tests kept teams of men living and working at 200-foot depths for thirty days; professional diver Jon Lindbergh (son of the Lone Eagle) went down to 432 feet for forty-nine hours; more than a dozen nonmilitary deep submersibles were operating, and numerous others were being built.

But the deep-diving craft soon proved too expensive to be widely used. Their hulls had to be precision-machined of high-quality steel or aluminum; otherwise they might spring a tiny leak, in which case water would shoot in at high pressure, instantly killing the aquanauts. Because of weight, even two-man subs needed elaborate buoyance controls, safety devices, and powerful motors to bring them up from a few hundred feet. In 1966 big manufacturers were predicting that by 1970 there would be a hundred-milion-dollar market for their undersea equipment, needed in setting up or repairing offshore oil-well operations, salvaging sunken vessels, laying pipes, repairing cables, building antisubmarine listening posts, prospecting for minerals, or just trying to find out what was in the immense, cold, dark regions under water. But these companies have been silent on the subject in recent years.

When we consider that those who talked about aquanauts' bright futures contemplated ventures no deeper than 500 feet, we needn't be surprised that little is known about nether regions of mountain lakes like Loch Ness, which is at least 750 feet deep—to say nothing of the even deeper lakes, fjords, channels, sounds, and inland sea basins within view of countless fishermen's settlements.

We live on the edges of a limbo into which we have never seen very far. Within it, unknown forms of life may thrive. Some creatures of the deeps may sometimes lie hidden in water within a few hundred feet of us, for all we know. To judge by talk in lakeside and seashore villages in various parts of the world—or by seamen's stories—monstrous things do indeed surface occasionally, only to submerge again.

Loch Ness tales are not unique. They are merely better known than similar tales about a number of other deep mountain waters in Scotland, Ireland, and other far northern countries. Certain deeps were said to be inhabited by monsters long before anyone thereabouts had heard of Loch Ness. Because these lochs and fjords are more isolated, there have been fewer witnesses, but some of their scattered reports are on record, and there is a remarkable consistency among most of them.

I went in search of evidence. I started at the two smaller lochs—Oich and Lochy—connected to Loch Ness by the Garry River and the Caledonian Canal, since I thought sea animals might make their way through them.

I found that the canal-bridge keeper at Loch Laggan had once seen some large thing rise to the surface beside his house and swim swiftly east toward Loch Ness. Also, I heard a tale about a deep pool in the river, below Oich Bridge. Local people call it the Children's Pool. According to the legend, one day many years ago, some children who lived at Inchlaggan were playing by the pool when a huge beast came out of the water and made its way up onto the bank. It seemed harmless, and the children were fearless. One scrambled onto its back—whereupon the creature lurched back into the water, and the child drowned.

"There is a tradition in the Great Glen of Scotland and indeed in Inverness generally that a strange beast inhabits the depth of Loch Oich," travel writer Alister MacGregor noted in 1937. "Although many of the natives and not a few travellers profess to have seen it, the beast has been overshadowed by its more famous neighbor in Loch Ness."

At Loch Lochy I saw a photograph in a family album, supposedly of a monster surfacing. It wasn't clear enough to prove anything—just a dark, irregular mass surrounded by foam. But I also heard that in 1930, before the Loch Ness Monster became famous, a man living in Lochyside warned his wife not to wash their linen in Loch Lochy anymore. When she pressed for a reason, he said that he had seen something ghastly and to his mind unnatural in the loch. He never said what it was.

Thirty years later Mr. and Mrs. Eric Robbins and a friend were startled by something in that same loch. First they saw two big waves spread across the still water. Then a fifteen-foot rounded back broke the surface, and began rolling over. Watching through binoculars, the trio glimpsed "a fin or paddle on its body as it turned." It made more waves, which broke on the beach at their feet. By then nine other people were watching. After a while the monster dived and was seen no more.

The River Lochy empties into Loch Arkaig. In 1857 Lord Malmesbury, an English statesman with lands in Scotland, wrote in his diary:

October 3rd. This morning my stalker and his boy gave me an account of a mysterious creature which they say exists in Loch Arkaig. It is the same animal of which one has occasionally read accounts in the newspapers as having been seen in Highland lochs, but hitherto the story has always been looked upon as fabulous. I am now, however, persuaded of its truth. My stalker, John Stuart, at Achnacarry, has seen it twice, both times when there was not a ripple on the water. Its head resembled that of a horse. It was also seen once by his three little children.

The Highlanders are very superstitious about this creature. I believe they think it has something diabolical in its nature, for when I said I wished I could get a shot at it, my stalker observed gravely, "Perhaps Your Lordship's gun would misfire."

To the west, another small but deep body of water, Loch Quoich, is also believed haunted. Once a laird was fishing there with two gillies when they saw a prodigious creature lying on the shore. The peer swore his servants to secrecy lest they all be thought drunk, but eventually gossip got around. Other Loch Quoich fishermen had seen something huge moving under water in times past.

Sir Walter Scott, who studied Highland lore, took the legendary water monsters seriously. In an 1815 letter to Lady Compton he wrote, "A monster long reported to inhabit Cauldshields Loch, a small sheet of water in this neighborhood, has of late been visible to sundry persons. . . . A very cool-headed, sensible man told me he had seen it in broad daylight." Sir Walter took his rifle with him when next he went strolling by the loch.

In quest of more evidence, I roamed the bleak, foggy Highlands, among steep mountains mirrored by large lakes where the local crofters are the only people to scan these remote gray reaches of water. Later I wandered south into Glencoe—the Glen of Weeping—and on through its mountainous west end, around the grim sentinels called the Nine Shepherds of Etive. Here and there I found lochs where monsters had supposedly been seen—sometimes long ago, sometimes in our own day.

As with Homer's Greeks and the jungle tribes of Africa, the Scottish settlements have preserved their past by word of mouth. Each village historian can recite several dozen stories, and is charged with keeping to their exact words. At Loch Fyne, a place near the sea, I heard a story of "a monstrous being in the loch" that terrorized residents in the sixteenth century. Several families built houses on a little isle in the loch, but were frightened off by a beast that crawled up from the water. I suppose anything as big as a plesiosaur or giant slug might do spectacular damage to flimsy wattle huts and young saplings.

Has such a brute ever appeared at Loch Fyne since the sixteenth century? The villagers won't say aye or nay. Whatever they may see swimming in their loch is not mentioned to strangers, I gather. But I did learn later, by consulting Edinburgh librarians, that in 1644 a Loch Fyne schoolmaster named James Gordan wrote that "the first inhabitants dwelling, as is reported, on one isle, were chased thence by a monster." And a Scottish history, *The Chronicles of Fortingale,* recorded that in 1570 "there was a monstrous fish seen in Loch Fyne, having a great eye in the head, and at times would stand above the water as high as the mast of a ship."

Allowing for exaggeration in transmittal through the centuries, this description might tally with the raised head and long neck mentioned so often in sightings at

Loch Ness. Similarly, there is a fourteenth-century map of Scotland, now in the Bodleian Library in Oxford, on which a note about Loch Ray is appended in Latin: "In this loch three wonders: a moving island, fish without fins, waves without wind."

Those same three wonders are credited to Loch Lomond in a 1653 atlas. I can imagine that a monster with a huge humped back but no visible head might seem from a distance to be an island; or might seem on closer view to be a kind of enormous fish without fins; and if only its wake were visible, as on the occasion of my own crew's lucky shot or the turmoil in Loch Lochy, it would indeed seem to be waves without wind.

Following the clue of the atlas, I went to Loch Lomond, Scotland's largest lake and the one most celebrated in song and story. There I heard a legend that in the eighteenth century a water animal with a body like that of a hippopotamus and a head like that of a horse sometimes manifested itself to villagers near the mouth of the River Enrick. An animal of this general description was reported twice in 1964: once by a Helensburgh couple named Haggerty, who saw "a long humped back" moving up the loch, and once by a railway engineer and a fireman, emerging in their locomotive from a tunnel onto a stretch of track above the loch, who saw something "like an overturned longboat, but moving fast through the water."

Suggestive, but inconclusive.

I next went to Great Britain's highest mountain, Ben Nevis—not very high by American standards, for it is only 4,406 feet. At its snowy foot lies Loch Treig, where especially fearsome monsters are said to live. In 1933 a hydroelectric project sent divers into it. Down there in the cold dark, where never a ray of light had shone nor a human being lived, they encountered some large moving body. Thereupon they rose to the surface at maximum safe speed, and quit their jobs. The Loch Treig people, like so many others, would not talk about the incident nor any later happenings, if there were such.

Over on Scotland's rocky west coast, around Loch Morar, the monster legends go back a long time. There is an ancient Scottish ballad:

> Morag, harbinger of death,
> Giant swimmer in deep-green Morar,
> The loch that has no bottom—
> There it is that Morag the monster lives.

"Who has not heard of the Morag?" a local writer, James MacDonald, asked rhetorically in 1907. He himself had seen it one January night in 1887, when he was crossing the loch to poach deer on the hills above Raitland. He saw its head and two humps. Then in 1895 Sir Theodore Brinckman and his wife were fishing on the loch with their stalker MacLaren, when Mrs. Brinckman thought she saw a long capsized boat several hundred yards away. "Could that be the launch we're expecting?" she asked. MacLaren said, "No, it'll just be the monster." And he explained to them that Morag the monster was well known, though seen only at intervals.

Loch Morar's shores have no houses. At 1,017 feet, it is the deepest lake in all the British Isles. There is a summer camp at Inverailort, and one day in 1946 a boatload of children from the camp were passing Bracorina Point on the north shore when one of them cried, "Look! What's that big thing on the bank?"

The steersman, Alexander MacDonnell, turned and saw an animal "about the size of an Indian elephant" flop off the rocks and into the water with a huge splash. (I think the long sinuous neck, rather like a trunk if you don't see the head, and the dark grayish color are what sometimes bring an elephant to people's minds when they try to describe the strange creatures from the lochs.)

In 1948 another boatload of tourists, from Liverpool, saw Morag swimming some distance behind their boat. Then nothing for twenty years. But in 1968 a local hotel worker, John MacVarish, was fishing when he saw its head and neck rise from the water. The neck was about five feet long, he thought, and about eighteen inches wide, tapering to a small flat head. It was moving fast, and the swirling water at its sides suggested paddling by broad flippers. When he started his engine to get nearer, the animal submerged.

Morag was seen three times in 1969. Twice it was on the white sandy bottom of Meoble Bay, where the water is clear and only sixteen feet deep. Trolling fishermen glimpsed it there—momentarily, because they gunned their motors and departed at first sight of it. The third encounter was more turbulent: On the evening of August 16, two Sunday fishermen, William Simpson and Duncan McDonnell, were rowing across Loch Morar's west end when they heard something and turned to see a large object moving toward them. A moment later their boat jolted, tilted up beneath them, then shuddered like a laboring engine. McDonnell used an oar to try to push the thing away; the body was heavy and solid to the touch. He saw the top of a snakelike head, about a foot across. He thought of giant cuttlefish known to exist in the middle depths of the Atlantic, and of the strange things sometimes found half digested in whales. He screamed.

The head turned. It was gruesome—huge tortoise eyes like saucers, a wide gash of a mouth. Meanwhile, Simpson had gotten hold of his shotgun, and fired wildly. The noise evidently frightened Morag. The bow of their boat came down, smacking the water with a boom like a cannon shot. Both men flew forward off their feet and fell flat in the boat. Another enormous slap behind them—then quiet. Morag had gone back to the depths.

Twice before, McDonnell had seen the monster, or some other: once a head and long neck, once a set of humps. He was reluctant to talk. Other people had tales to tell, he said, but they would not speak for fear of being laughed at.

His own caution was learned hard. He had told a wire-service man about the skirmish with Morag, only to see it wildly exaggerated in a news story published around the world. According to the story, the monster bit off the end of the oar, and Simpson's gunshot blasted a four-inch hole in its flank.

No one has seen Morag at close range since the shooting, although a Loch Morar survey set up watches along the shore in the summers of 1970, '71, and '72. Members of the expeditions did sight a large hump three times, and once missed getting a photograph by only an instant. The full account of their investigations, as well as the historical background, is reported in the 1972 book *The Search for Morag,* by Elizabeth Montgomery Campbell and David Solomon.

I took a boat from the coast to the Hebrides Islands, and found monster stories there too. During their tour of the Hebrides in 1773, Boswell and Johnson visited the small island of Rasay, whose "gloom of desolation" put Johnson in a foul mood. Boswell recorded a story their guide told them as they passed a loch:

> He said there was a wild beast in it, which came and devoured a man's daughter. . . . The man with a red-hot spit destroyed it. Malcolm [the guide] showed me the man's little hiding place. He did not laugh when he told me this story.

The big somber island called Skye was the scene of a determined effort to capture a water monster believed to live in Loch nan Dubhrachan. According to Mary Donaldson, a Skye writer who heard of it from an old man, in 1870 the local laird tried dragging the loch for the creature, atfer seeing it on the shore once. A school holiday was declared for the occasion, crowds arrived by dog carts and two-wheel carriages, and "there was more whiskey than at a funeral." Two boats dragged the loch with a long net that may or may not have reached the bottom. When it caught on a snag, the crowd stampeded off, thinking the monster had been netted. The laird caught only two pike.

The island of Lewis, northernmost of the Outer Hebrides, contains Loch Suainbhal; for decades people threw lambs into this loch to feed some creature believed to live in its depths. This loch was the scene of incidents reported in the London *Times* for March 6, 1856. Tucked discreetly at the bottom of an inside page, an article headed THE SEA SERPENT IN THE HIGHLANDS said:

> The village of Leurbost, Parish of Lochs, Lewis, is at present the scene of an unusual occurrence. This is no less than the appearance in one of the inland fresh-water lakes of an animal which from its great size and dimensions has not a little puzzled our island naturalists.
>
> It has been repeatedly seen within the last fortnight by crowds of people, many of whom have come from the remotest parts of the parish to witness the uncommon spectacle. The animal is described by some as being in appearance and size like "a large peat stack," while others affirm that a six-oared boat could pass between the huge fins, which are occasionally visible.

This seems to be the very first newspaper mention of the strange lake monsters that have been legendary in Scotland for so long. In Scottish folklore they were called kelpies, which means a watery ghost or specter, usually in the form of a horse. We've seen how the long necks and heads reported in so many sightings are similar to those of horses. "Every lake has its kelpie or water-horse, often seen by the shepherd," noted an early travel writer. "[It may be] dashing along the surface of the deep, or browsing . . . on its verge."

Tim Dinsdale's book *The Leviathans* lists multiple monster sightings in Loch Linnhe, Loch Eil, and Loch Shiel. These lochs are in or around the Great Glen. But I didn't take time to visit them. I had heard enough about Scotland's mysterious beasts, I decided, and it was time to visit other lands of deep water to learn whether similar—or dissimilar—creatures had been seen.

Legends of aquatic monsters are a curiously common motif in early Irish literature. Ireland's lake apparitions are sometimes called "direful wurrms." Hearing this, I thought of the famous sea serpents, which I'll discuss in the next chapter. No Irishman can forget the sea. Even in the center of Ireland, sea gulls follow the plow. In that weird, wet Atlantic light, the remote past seems vivid, and ghosts and legends become believable. Maybe the sea really spawned this island's mythical lake spirits.

But I thought otherwise after a few days in Ireland. In our own lifetime the monsters have been asserting themselves, and people who have supposedly seen them are inclined to think them less like serpents or colossal worms than like Scotland's humped-back, barrel-bodied, long-necked, python-headed anomalies.

South of Clifden in the province of Connacht, there is a wide bogland in which a stream connects a chain of three small lakes with the sea. In 1954 Mrs. Georgina Carberry, with three companions, was fishing in Lough Fadda, the largest of these lakes. They saw "a black object which moved slowly, showing two humps. The head was about three feet out of water, in a long curve." It swung around and dived.

Another time, Pat Walsh was in his boat on that same lake when a head and neck emerged from the water near him. He rowed ashore at top speed.

And there was the time when a family of seven watched "a black animal about twelve feet long," with the usual hump and neck, swimming around the lake. On a fourth occasion a local shepherd saw a monster on land near the lake.

Because of all this, enthusiastic Irish monster hunters made an all-out effort to capture whatever lurked in Lough Fadda. A bold skindiver went down. Nets were cast. Underwater charges of gelignite were set off. All three lakes in the chain proved surprisingly shallow, and were searched avidly. The thing in Lough Fadda, if there really had been one, must have escaped down the stream to the sea.

The Shannon River is Ireland's chief inland waterway. I wouldn't expect a monster to be comfortable in such a busy stream. But the river flows through several big lakes. In one, Lough Ree, above Athlone, several disquieting incidents have occurred during the last quarter century.

In 1950 a cabin cruiser thudded against something in the middle of the channel, where the water had always been thought to be deep. The startled skipper took bearings to fix the spot, and it was soon dragged. Nothing was found. Nevertheless, charts of the Shannon now mark the spot "Unidentified Snag." The water there is seventy feet deep.

One summer evening, two men walking along the shore saw an animal swimming. Its neck was a foot above the surface, then there was a gap of water, and then a black hump. They thought it must be a calf, and put out in a boat to rescue it. But it submerged before they reached it. The beast could not have been a calf, because cattle keep their heads and necks down level with the water when swimming, as dogs do.

Paddy Hanley, a retired postman whose parents came from the Black Islands in the middle of the lough, remembers a boyhood scare there. He and some of his family were fishing north of Yew Point when he hooked something. His fishing line was the strongest kind—"almost a rope," he said. The boat was pulled clear across the lake, past the Adelaide buoy, before he cut the line. He never saw what he had hooked. But he has heard of similar incidents over the years.

In February 1960 two net fishermen, Pat Ganley and Joseph Quigly, felt their net hauling something huge and heavy. While they were trying to drag it up, the net broke and the creature escaped. This happened in the middle of the lough, in sixty feet of water.

The best-documented Lough Ree sighting that I know of was made by three Dublin priests during the sunny, still afternoon of May 18, 1960. They were fishing on the loch, which they knew well from previous trips, and were watching for rising trout when Father Matt Burke muttered to his companions, "Do you see what I see?"

All three saw some large animal only a hundred yards away. "It went down under the water and came up again in the form of a loop," Father Daniel Murray said later. "There was about eighteen inches of head and neck over the water. It was getting its propulsion from underneath, and we didn't see all of it. We watched it moving along the surface for two or three minutes. Then it submerged gradually. Another couple of minutes later it reappeared, still following the same course. . . . It reached a point thirty yards offshore, where it submerged, and we saw it no more."

The vocation of these viewers at least assured attention for their tale. They had nothing to gain—and perhaps a little respect to lose—by telling it. To make their seriousness clear, they submitted a detailed written account to the Inland Fisheries Trust.

They also crossed the lake to talk with Colonel Harry Rice, a well-known authority on the Shannon River. In his book about the river, *Thanks for the Memory,* he had mentioned a monster supposed to haunt Lough Ree. He himself had never seen any monster, but a friend of his said that it looked "for all the world like barrels strung together," presumably a reference to humps. Colonel Rice wrote later:

> I took down everything they said. . . . I cross-examined the priests for almost two hours, and applied all the criticisms one would normally use, but two of them were so convinced that they had seen something extraordinary, that I could not shake them. . . . These gentlemen are expert fishermen, and thoroughly qualified to observe.

These stories from Lough Ree have an odd resonance, because they echo a line from the saga of the legendary Irish hero Finn MacCool. About three centuries before the time of Christ, it is said, Finn battled with numerous monsters and slew them all. "He slew a phantom and a serpent on Loch Ree," the bard recounted casually, in reciting a long list of Finn's deeds. The saga gives no details.

I found enough evidence to convince me that there may well be, in some Irish lakes, powerful dragons like those seen intermittently in Scotland. Perhaps there will never be convincing photographs of them; now we see them, now we don't, and we would have to be very quick with a camera to shoot one at close range before it disappeared again.

The Scandinavians, I find, have taken lake monsters for granted since time immemorial. In 1765 a British correspondent noted in *The Gentleman's Magazine,* "The people of Stockholm report that a great dragon named Necker infests the neighboring lake." Because of this, he wrote, they tried to dissuade the visiting bishop of Avranches from swimming in Lake Mälaren one hot summer day. The doughty French cleric would not be deterred. The Swedes "were greatly surprised when they saw him return."

Although Bishop Huet didn't believe in Necker, I think descendants of that monster may still dwell in some of Sweden's ninety-six thousand icy lakes. There are well-authenticated reports from a lake called Storsjön in the heart of the country. The lake covers 176 square miles—a small lake for Sweden—and is frozen in winter. But it is nearly nine hundred feet deep, and its middle levels are probably no colder than Loch Ness.

On the island of Forso in this lake, there is an ancient stone carved with a runic inscription and a sketch of a beast with a long neck and flippers. At the lake's east shore is the town of Östersund, where I visited a museum containing harpoons and some enormous spring traps. These were used in 1894, records show, in a sustained effort to catch the monster. The curator, in a letter to Tim Dinsdale, said that the creature seemed most active from 1820 to 1898, when "mostly trustworthy persons" saw it twenty-two times.

Something still lives in Lake Storsjön, according to the people of Östersund. As recently as the summer of 1965 they saw it several times. In the methodical Swedish manner, they compiled a description that is more detailed than anything available from Loch Ness. "The head is said to be round and smooth, with great eyes," the curator wrote. "The extremities are described as short, stumpy legs or feet, possibly big clumsy fins, possibly long, webbed hind legs."

Even more methodically, Norwegians in various towns have held court proceedings to try to pin down facts about monsters seen in their lakes. Witnesses' sworn testimony was taken down verbatim. One such court was held at Mandel in 1867, and another at Stavanger in 1892. As usual, local scientists who had seen nothing came forward to assert that the eyewitnesses must be mistaken: no such monsters could conceivably exist, and those who claimed to have seen a live creature were fools or drunks who had merely seen masses of sawdust or vegetation. The court investigations reached no conclusions.

"It has always seemed very curious to me," wrote the noted English zoologist Gerald Durrell, "that anybody faced with reasonably good evidence . . . as to the possible existence of a creature as yet unknown to science, should not throw up their hands in delight at even the faintest chance of such a windfall in the shrinking world. Unfortunately the opposite is generally the case. Man suddenly leaves you bereft of speech at the lengths to which he will go to prove that nothing new can exist. . . . There has been an endless succession of arrogant people who adopt the same blinkered attitude."

I counted twenty-six different lakes in Sweden, Norway, and Iceland where monsters have reportedly been seen. One of them is even named Monster's Lake—Ormsjoen. But nearly all these lakes are fingers of the sea, so I couldn't be sure whether the creatures might be sea serpents or the plesiosaurlike monsters that seem to prefer semilandlocked lakes. So I'll reserve consideration of them until the next chapter.

Russian peasants, like other far-northern folk, have tales of huge creatures seen in their lakes. Soviet scientists are more disposed to pay attention than are their Western counterparts—particularly since some sightings have been by scientists.

In July 1953 a geologist, V. A. Tverdokhlebov, was

leading a crew on a survey of a plateau in northeast Siberia. They reached Lake Vorota, about seventy-five miles from the nearest village, on a sunny windless day. The geologist and his assistant, Boris Bashkator, saw what they thought was an oil drum floating in the lake about three hundred yards out. Then they were amazed to see the thing swim toward shore. They climbed a cliff face for a better (or safer?) view, and saw a large head with wide-set eyes—much too big for a giant turtle.

"The animal was moving itself forward in leaps, its upper part at times appearing above water and then disappearing," the geologist wrote. "At a distance of 100 meters from shore it stopped. It began to beat the water vigorously, raising a cascade of spray, then plunged out of sight." They watched for a long time, but it did not surface again.

Another lake on the same Sordongnakh Plateau has been explored by Soviet aqualung divers seeking a monster reported by two different scientific expeditions. They never got close to it, although once they did see three large rounded objects in motion. They ran along the shore trying to photograph these, without success. They weren't sure whether it was one animal with three humps, or three animals swimming together.

There is better evidence from Lake Khaiyr, deep in the tundra of Siberia's Yanski region. A biologist named Nikita Gladkikh "literally ran into" a monster on the shore, according to an article in *Komsomolskaya Pravda* by G. Rukosuyer, deputy leader of the geological survey to which Gladkikh was attached. The huge thing had crawled up into the grass. It had a small head on a long gleaming neck, and a great black-skinned body.

Horrified, the biologist ran to alert his colleagues. When they got to the lake with cameras and rifles, the thing was gone, but they did see a large swath of trampled grass. As if to vouch for Gladkikh's credibility, a monster later surfaced in the middle of the lake. The leader of the expedition and two assistants saw it—a head high out of the water, and a thrashing tail that produced big waves. The Soviets are still investigating. Perhaps they will be the ones to produce final proof of lake monsters.

Many Indian tribes of North America believed in monsters or powerful spirits that lived in deep lakes. The belief is still strong among some surviving tribes in Canada, where the country is sprinkled with hundreds of thousands of lakes like puddles drying in the sun between the Great Lakes and the Arctic Circle.

Among the largest of these is Lake Okanagan in British Columbia, an area that was cut off from the sea only recently, geologically speaking. It covers about 127 square miles. The Shuswap Indians who live in the Okanagan Valley are in awe of it. Until a century ago they made ritual offers of chickens and puppies to Naitaka, the monster spirit who, they believed, dwelt in its dark forbidding depths. They gave the name of Monster's Island to a small rocky isle in the center of Okanagan.

The prehistoric Shuswaps in that area left crude drawings of Naitaka cut in stone, showing the familiar long neck and flippers. Their dread didn't fade away with the advent of white settlers, because sometimes these newcomers too saw apparitions in the lake. In 1854 two horses, swimming across the lake beside their owner in a canoe, suddenly sank. The half-breed canoeist claimed that they had been pulled down by some strong force.

Decades later, a settler named John McDougal saw the same thing happen to a pair of his horses, towing him across in a boat. If he had not cut them loose, he said, his boat would have been pulled down too.

The whites' name for the monster is now Ogopogo, a fake Indian name made up by a music-hall comedian when he sang extemporaneous verses about the creature in Vernon one night in 1924. The name stuck.

Ogopogo, or Naitaka, has been seen occasionally in recent decades—sometimes a black hump, sometimes a series of humps gliding along, sometimes a "goatlike" head on a long neck. In July 1952 three women sighted it from the lawn of a house at Kelowna.

One of the women, a visitor from Vancouver, later wrote:

> I am a stranger here. I did not even know such things existed. But I saw it so plainly. A head like a horse that reared right out of the water. The coils glistened. . . . It was so beautiful, with the sun shining on it. It came up three times, then submerged and disappeared.

In the summer of 1959 the creature was seen on three different days: on July 20 by the owner of the Vernon *Advertiser,* who got close in his motorboat before it submerged; on August 12 by the rector of the Anglican church in Penticton, who peered from the porch of his cottage at Narmanta; and a few days later by Mr. and Mrs. Bruce Miller, who saw it from their car and pulled up to watch.

In 1960 the German vice-consul in Vancouver happened to visit the lake and see "a spoil of waves with white foam, like the wash of a boat moving swiftly, but there was no boat." In 1963 a local fisherman saw three humps slither past his boat from a weed-choked corner.

In 1964 a teen-ager named Kenny Unser was playing with his dog near an old wharf in Kelowna, throwing sticks into the water for the dog to fetch. Suddenly he saw a wave. Then three feet of dark tail rose above the water and slapped hard, splashing the wharf. Kenny ran for his life. I was reminded of old tales of Naitaka's appetite for puppies and ferocity toward horses. Despite the apparent shyness of lake monsters, some of them may be dangerous when hungry.

There is other monster lore at other Canadian lakes. Lake Shuswap seems to have a creature that the Indians call Tazama. In nearby Lake Cowichan there is said to be something known as the Tsinqaw. Something else is said to lurk in Lake Pohengamok. The Crees say that a serpentine thing lives in Lake Meminisha in Ontario.

In Quebec, reports of a monster at Mocking Lake

persisted for so many years that the director of the provincial fish and game commission went there to investigate. He found many witnesses but no proof.

Similarly persistent reports came from lonely Lake Manitoba. In 1908 and 1909 trappers said they saw a monster there. Every few years someone else was frightened by something in the lake. Finally in 1957 the minister of industry and commerce sent a team to search the lake. They found nothing, but the reports continued. On August 12, 1960, seventeen people on the beach saw three great animals in the water.

Canadian scientists, like Russians, seem more open-minded than their colleagues in other countries. Professor James A. MacLeod, chairman of the University of Manitoba's zoology department, organized expeditions to the lake in 1960 and 1961. He gave up in 1962—and probably has cursed his luck ever since, for in August of that year a monster was actually photographed by two fishermen, Richard Vincent and John Konefell, from an outboard motorboat.

"We first spotted the object about three hundred yards away," Vincent told newsmen. "After swinging into the direction it was heading, we saw what we believed to be a large black snake which was swimming with a ripple action. . . . It was about a foot in girth, and about twelve feet of the monster was above water. No head was visible."

They estimated that the hump shown in their photograph was about two feet long. The gunwale of the boat is visible, giving perspective that indicates that the object was about fifty yards away when they photographed it. But it speeded up, and their motorboat could get no closer.

Dr. MacLeod judged the photograph genuine. "If that isn't the monster, I'd like to know what the deuce it is," he said.

Certainly it resembles creatures described in many of the reports from Scotland, Ireland, Scandinavia, Russia, and Canada. The photograph simply shows a blurred, rounded section and a white crescent of foam.

more than frightening figments of imagination. The evidence may not be conclusive, but it is fairly consistent—and voluminous as well as long-continuing. Sooner or later, I believe, we'll know for sure that some creatures survived from the age of the dinosaurs, and have lived and bred in the dark depths of mountain lakes for millions of years.

7

Sea Giants

Huge unidentified entities sometimes arise in the sea. At least, the idea that they do so has been held by many people, for centuries if not since the dawn of history.

Such an idea is the main proposition of the earliest piece of written literature in English, and in fact in all Teutonic literature—the saga of Beowulf, who slays two ogrelike water-dwelling monsters and thereafter rules a coastal kingdom for fifty years. Scholars find that this epic came from known history of the sixth century in Denmark, fused with Norse legends and finally written down by an anonymous monk around 700 A.D.

Scandinavian folklore also immortalizes other monsters. There was the serpent-dragon Fafnir, killed by Sigurd—the legendary Siegfried of German tradition, the hero whom Wagner's operas celebrated. There was the myth of the god Thor fishing for the huge Midgard serpent. There were the monsters with long serpentine necks carved as figureheads of Viking longships. (One famous ship was called the *Sea Dragon*.) Ancient plaques found at Uland in Sweden portray warriors battling monsters.

Were these maritime terrors mere figments of imagination?

Zoologists and paleontologists and other landlubbers used to think so, but discoveries during the past century have pushed many myths into the realm of possibility.

For example, the once-fabled Scandinavian horrors called kraken are now known to exist. As I mentioned in chapter 4, they are gigantic squids. This had to be admitted in 1873, after one attacked a boatload of Newfoundland fishermen, who managed to hack off a tentacle. Measured on shore, the tentacle was nineteen feet long and three inches thick. Squids weighing as much as four thousand pounds were found later, and marine biologists no longer insist that these must be the biggest squids in the depths.

But what of Scandinavia's other legendary water giant, the skrimsl? A skrimsl—sea serpent—is recorded to have surfaced during the summer of 1345 and again in 1749 in Iceland, twice more in 1819, and again in 1860. The skrimsl is no squid. This is clear from the extant accounts. They mention a horselike head, a long arching neck, and humps with water between.

I've been in Iceland. It's a wild, glacial, silent island, a moonscape half submerged in icy water. The sea has the flat, black look of great depth. The remote people, farmers and fishermen though they are, have always valued learning—hence the preservation of their old skrimsl reports.

The 1345 sighting was reported in the *Icelandic Chronicle* with sober restraint: "At times there appeared humps . . . with water between them. No one knows the dimensions of the creature, for none saw its head or tail. Consequently there is no certainty as to what it was." The establishment would assume it was turtles or dolphins in a line. But today's Icelanders suspect that it was a skrimsl—mainly because the later sightings, reported by more people who were more sure of what they saw, concur with the early ones.

The 1749 manifestation was reported in the *Thjoth Sogur*, which quoted descriptions by a lawyer named Peter and two others:

They described it as moving rapidly. These men, after watching it for some time, came at dusk to Arneither-stede, where they mentioned what they had seen.

While they were speaking the monster rose to the surface in front of the farm. It appeared to be very long and showed one large hump.

All the farm people, without exception, at Arnei-ther-stede saw the creature.

Soon afterward something with three humps astonished everyone at Hrafnagorthis. They watched prudently from the beach while it frolicked offshore all day. In 1819 a long creature, humps undulating, surfaced off Arneither-stede again, and is said to have gone ashore on the little isle of Grimsey, where it left deep blurry marks in the sand.

The Reverend Sabine Baring-Gould and his wife toured Iceland in 1860. One evening he wrote in his journal:

To our great delight we met at Skogkotr with Martin and the Yankee. They had been fishing. They were full of the appearance of a Skrimsl, a half-fabulous monster which has generally been considered the offspring of the imagination.

My two friends had arrived only the day after the monster had been seen disporting itself on the surface, and they were able to obtain some curious information. One morning the farmer and his household had observed something unusual, and presently were able to descry a large head like that of a seal rising out of the water. Behind this appeared a back or a hump, and after an interval of water, a second hump. The creature moved slowly and seemed to be enjoying the sun.

When Baring-Gould got back to Reykjavik, he met a local scientist, a Dr. Hjaltalin, who said that a great mass of meat and bones had once been found on a local beach. The bones were entirely unlike whalebones, the doctor said—in fact, they were unlike bones of any animal he knew. He had no time to study them, for the huge corpse was making itself too noticeable under the summer sun, and townspeople towed it out to sea.

This was neither the first nor the last unidentifiable

monster cast up by the surf, only to be found highly undesirable and quickly recommitted. In 1808 at Stronsay, one of the Orkney Islands, there was found —and scrutinized briefly—a hulking thing "without the least resemblance or affinity to fish," according to a paper by Dr. John Barclay in the journal of Edinburgh's Wernerian Natural History Society.

He had collected affidavits by Stronsay residents who said there were three pairs of stumpy fins, flippers, or the like. Nevertheless, a noted British anatomist examined two vertebrae that had been preserved, and pronounced the monster to have been merely an oversized shark. Even so, Orkney fishermen of today, who are notably stolid and matter-of-fact, "all know and accept sea serpents," according to Ivan T. Sanderson, a leading naturalist and author.

The New Zealand *Times* of March 19, 1883, reported that bones of an unidentified animal about forty feet long had been found on the Queensland coast and taken to the nearest town, Rockhampton. A hip bone of the creature was described as enormous. Now, it so happens that whales' hip bones are vestigial, about one foot long. There appears to be no record of what the experts at Rockhampton thought of, or did with, the strange bones. Perhaps they hid them in a box in a storeroom, as American paleontologists did with the first dinosaur fossils dug up in 1820.

Still another imposing mass, perhaps similar to the Orkney one, drifted ashore in 1896 twelve miles south of St. Augustine, Florida. At first appendages on it were said to be stumps of tentacles. However, since the mass was four and a half feet high, seven feet wide, and twenty-one feet long, with an estimated weight of seven tons, it couldn't have been a giant squid; they aren't this big. The New York *Herald* of December 2 reported, "The hide is light pink, nearly white, and in the sunshine has a distinct silvery appearance. It is very tough and cannot be penetrated even with a sharp knife." Sharp knives can of course cut whale meat. Unimpressed by the discernible facts, Professor A. E. Verrill wrote in the *American Naturalist* that the thing must be part of a sperm whale, even though he admitted that its head had no features of the head of any known sperm whale.

Before the days of deep-sea dredging, scientists reasoned that no life could exist far down in the sea. Whales were thought to spend their lives near the surface, since they held their breath while under water. But in 1932 the cable repair ship *All America* raised a broken transoceanic cable from a depth of 3,240 feet. Entangled in it was a dead sperm whale 45 feet long. There went another of the certitudes of marine biology.

Seals too are now known to dive phenomenally deep in quest of food. Their stomachs have yielded the bones of a species of fish that has never been seen alive; in fact, even its remains are unknown except in the stomachs of seals. Ichthyologists classify it as part of a group that typically inhabits the deeper ocean trenches.

How can seals and whales endure the tremendous pressure changes involved in dives of several thousand feet? Nobody knows. These are warm-blooded mammals, like man. When human divers surface from a dive too fast, they are afflicted with "the bends," caused by swift concentration of nitrogen bubbles in the blood with sudden release of pressure. This dissolved nitrogen comes fizzing out in the blood like soda bubbles in a bottle of pop when the cap is removed, and can clog the veins, rupture organs, cause excruciating pain, and even kill a diver who comes up quickly from two hundred feet or so. Theoretically, the same fate should befall a seal, a whale, or any unknown deep-sea mammal that surfaced suddenly.

During a stay aboard Jacques Cousteau's research vessel *Calypso,* I witnessed firsthand the awesome diving capabilities of the sperm whale. We had ventured out of Djibouti, the last bastion of the French Foreign Legion, to hunt the Red Sea for pods of sperm whales. We hoped to film a study of their behavior for use in the Cousteau television series.

In the early summer months the peripatetic families of sperms proliferated in the region. The spring crop of babies traveled with the pods. It was the presence of the newborn that had lured us to the Red Sea. Cousteau had said that his observations in the past convinced him that infant sperm whales did not possess deep-diving capability. Apparently the skill or physical development needed to sound is not innate.

Our observations during the filming confirmed this fact. When we affixed a line with a marker buoy to a large female whale, she immediately sounded, taking almost a mile of line straight down. Her baby, on the other hand, simply could not sound. After almost forty-eight hours of the baby "on the line," we witnessed an extraordinary event. The mother and a second large sperm whale squeezed the baby between them and sounded, carrying the baby deep enough to break the line we had attached.

As to how whales accomplish their remarkable diving feats, we are still in the dark. We do know that from great depths, where whales endure pressure of a thousand pounds on every square inch of their bodies, they rise again like express elevators.

One conceivable explanation is that the whale, unlike the human diver, doesn't breathe through an air hose while diving. The air supply held in his gigantic lungs may not force enough nitrogen into his blood to harm him. Another possibility is that waxy or fatty substances called spermaceti may get into the whale's respiratory system in the form of a waxy foam; these substances can soak up six times as much nitrogen as blood can.

"The plain truth is, however, that we really do not know," writes Rachel Carson in *The Sea Around Us*. "It is obviously impossible to confine a whale and experiment on him, and almost as difficult to dissect a dead one satisfactorily."

The crushing weight of water at great depths doesn't hurt fragile creatures like the glass sponge and the jellyfish. This miracle seems even more perplexing when we know the facts about pressure in the ocean. At sea level, the pressure of air on any living body is about one "atmosphere," or fifteen pounds to the square inch of surface. At the limit of diving-helmet range, the pressure is about forty-five pounds on each square inch of a man's body. This variation of three atmospheres is about as much as an unprotected human body can withstand.

However, for creatures at home in the depths, the saving fact is that the pressure inside their tissues is the same as that outside. While this balance is kept, they are no more harmed by pressures of a ton or more than we are by ordinary air pressure.

This explains the survival of creatures that live out their whole lives on the bottom or in any other particular depth zone. But the real miracle, still unexplained, is the ability of some forms of life to zip up and down through many levels of pressure. The tiny plankton do this daily; whales, likewise; thus, also—at least occasionally—do the still-unclassified giants in very deep lakes as well as the ocean depths.

Such creatures possess some mysterious attribute lacking in other deep-water species. Abrupt changes of water pressure are lethal to fish that have built-in air bladders, as anyone knows who has seen a trawler's net raised from six hundred feet or more. Even when such fish avoid nets, they sometimes stray above the zone to which they are adjusted and find themselves unable to get down again. In the lessened compression of upper waters, the gas in the bladder expands, making them more buoyant. They probably try to fight their way down again, opposing the upward pull with all their strength. If they lose the fight, they "fall" to the surface, injured and dying, as the abrupt release of pressure lets their tissues distend and burst.

But to the strange aquatic denizens known vaguely as sea serpents and sea monsters, sunny air on the surface is presumably just as acceptable as the perpetual darkness and pulverizing pressures they apparently endure for long periods under water. There is no indication that they dwell in zones only a few hundred feet down. If they did, they would almost certainly have been detected by divers, submarines, or sonar beams. Oceanographers have by now explored in detail all the comparatively shallow zones of the seas, and have classified everything they noted therein.

But the depths have barely been looked into.

Leonard Engel, a distinguished scientific writer, recently pointed out:

> We are far from having finished cataloging the kinds of things that live there. Almost anything can be expected from the sea.
>
> It may be presumptuous to rule out sea monsters entirely. . . . A research vessel did get hold of something 1,200 feet down that was large enough to bend a three-foot iron hook and escape.
>
> Other large creatures lurk in the gathering darkness. . . . There is something down at 3,000 feet, a sizable something that has been detected by explosive sonic methods, but nobody yet knows what it is or how big it is. So far, it is simply a squiggle on photographic paper.

Eavesdropping on the underwater world with the help of hydrophones, scientists have recorded a wide variety of noises made by living things. At depths of a mile or more, the sounds are loud and strange and unassociated with anything in aquariums; they suggest coal rattling down a chute, steaks sizzling, a loose bearing in an engine, the dull roll of a soft-shoe dancer atop an empty barrel, a band saw rasping through sheet metal.

One type of monster down there might be a giant eel. A Danish research ship once picked up an eel larva that was three feet long. If it were in the same proportion to adult eels as larvae of other species are, it would grow to ninety feet at maturity.

It is not inconceivable that some monsters might be a kind of eel, and others a variant of the antediluvian plesiosaur, and others an offshoot of seals or dolphins that evolved a long neck and huge body; all monsters do not necessarily belong to the same family.

Ever since man first went down to the sea in ships, sailors have returned with tales of strange behemoths plying the waves. Ships change through the ages, but the sea doesn't. During man's comparatively brief dominance of the land, how many strange beasts have been dragged from the sea or found on beaches, and either dumped back because they had no commercial value or boiled down because they had?

In that unchanging environment, amphibious mammals or reptiles might easily maintain themselves undetected at great depths for millions of years. We already know that creatures from that age are still with us—crocodiles and turtles, for example.

Despite all these possibilities, the hypothetical sea monsters have probably ignited more controversy—some of it wonderfully acrimonious—than any other creature ever reported on land or sea. Concrete evidence of their existence—aside from statements by people claiming to have seen them—is scanty, and I've sketched nearly all of it in the preceding pages. However, supposedly open-minded scientists continue to proclaim the impossibility of any species that they've never seen; old-line savants still deduce, merely from the lack of specimens in captivity or in museums, that no unnamed monster can exist anywhere.

"There are no sea serpents," a leading ichthyologist said, according to the *Saturday Evening Post*. "The trouble is that too many people see things, then don't know how to describe what they saw." This attitude seems fairly typical of the position taken by a sizable segment of the scientific community.

However much it may be scoffed at, dismissed as an invention of promoters, or explained away as seaweed and driftwood and processions of dolphins, the great unknown of the seas has been reported by so many reliable witnesses that I think it must be accepted as reality. Anyone scanning the data with at least a half-open mind will conclude that we cannot write off sea monsters for lack of credible evidence, even though the evidence consists mainly of eyewitness testimony.

It can be shown that a well-defined if nightmarish sea creature has been reported from somewhere almost every year since 1800. There is a remarkable similarity

In Search of
Myths
and
Monsters

Why did so many people believe in composite half-human mixtures like the sphinx. Was there a living model?

Modern expedition in search of Villcabamba in Peru. The ancient Incans were horrified upon first seeing Spaniards on horseback. They thought the horse and man were one.

Knossos. The mythical bull-man Minotaur
stood for the King of Knossos while the King
impersonated the Semitic bull-god El.

Hunedoara Castle where Dracula was reputed to have lived.

Prince Vlad "Dracula" of Walachia (Romania) had a reputation for wholesale and hideous executions in the 15th century. This authentic historical Dracula made the fictional one seem tame.

Sragov Church where Dracula is buried.

A fish that couldn't be—a coalacanth.
The commonest small fish in the
Devonian era (about 5 inches long), the
coalacanth presumably became extinct
70 million years ago. Yet, in 1938 a
descendant, more than 5 feet long,
was pulled up in a fisherman's net.

Other coalacanths were later caught and the angle of
fins varied as much as 180 degrees between one
fish and another. The first amphibians developed from
coalacanths. This may shed new light on how fins evolved
into arms and legs as fish began spending time ashore.

Stories of a monster in Loch Ness stretch back through 14 centuries of oral tradition and written reference.

Is the Loch Ness monster the ghost of a great dinosaur. The giant aquatic reptiles called plesiosaurs are similar to many eyewitness accounts of the Loch Ness monster.

Unidentified sea object. This mass drifted ashore in 1896
near St. Augustine, Florida. It was 4½ feet high, 7 feet
wide and 21 feet long, with an estimated weight of 7 tons.

St. Augustine Historical Society

Dr. Grover Krantz,
a physical anthropologist, did
a buildup from plaster casts
of Bigfoot footprints.

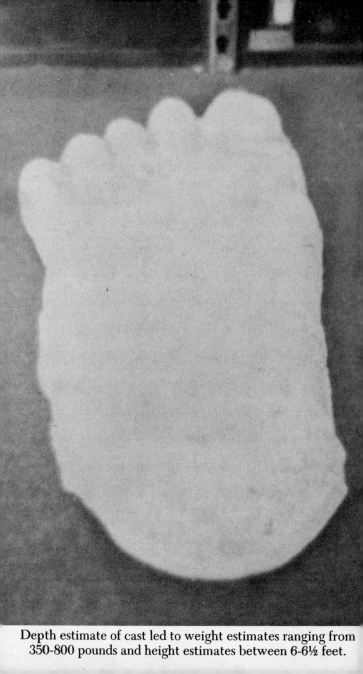

Depth estimate of cast led to weight estimates ranging from 350-800 pounds and height estimates between 6-6½ feet.

Cabin in Ape Canyon where Bigfoot was sighted.

Peter Byrne, a Bigfoot
hunter, makes a track cast.
Byrne is in charge of
the Bigfoot Information
Center, The Dalles, Oregon.

Monsters are said to guard Honey Swamp in Mississippi.

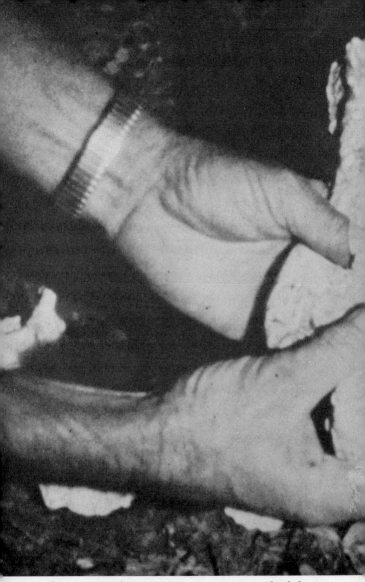

Plaster cast of Honey Swamp monster which has been described as a skunk-ape.

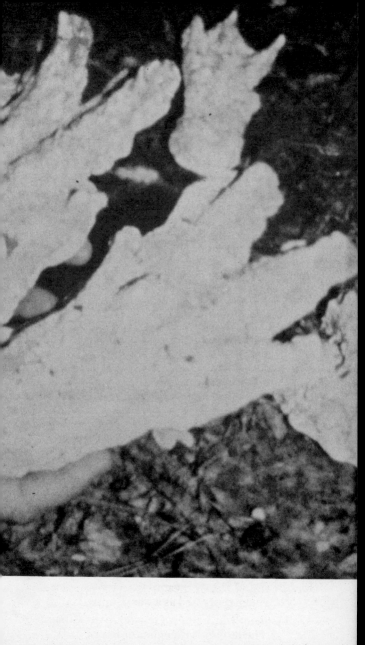

Of the giant lizards, only a few relatives remain.
The largest is the monitor lizard,
the Komodo dragon, growing up to 12 feet long.

If there never were dragons, why did the thought
of an imaginary one seem so evil to
civilizations already old before the Bible was written?

Dr. Norman Gary went to Brazil to test the aggressiveness of the killer bees. All that was required to arouse the bees was to dangle a black leather patch at the hive entrance.

Killer bees and honey bees common in the United States are
nearly identical. If the killer bees continue
their northward migration from South America at 200 miles
a year, they could reach the U.S. by 1990.

Genetic experiments are being attempted to take the killer instinct out of the killer bee. Drones, representing the gentle European variety, are collected from special hives.

In the laboratory, drones are drained of semen and an anesthetized killer queen is prepared for artificial insemination. The queen is then introduced into a hive. If the experiment is successful, the queen's eggs will bear a gentler bee.

among many reports made by isolated people who never heard of one another or their reports.

It is a striking fact that most people who admit to having seen sea monsters are Englishmen or Scots or Scandinavians, or particularly New Englanders and Newfoundlanders—seafaring people even if well educated. These regional folk are known as conservative, skeptical, and grimly honest. Why are these virtually the only groups that lay claim to sightings of sea monsters? Possibly because they are the kind of people who can stand up to the ridicule that comes from affirming an unpopular belief.

Let's consider the earliest sighting that is well authenticated by a formidable body of witnesses: the famous events of August 1817, when Massachusetts saw a "sea serpent."

One day during that month the skipper of a coastal vessel, forced into Gloucester by bad weather, made a strange statement in the town auction room. At the harbor entrance, he said gravely, he and his crew had seen an awful beast that looked like a serpent—sixty feet long. He was laughed out of the room.

But in two weeks Gloucester was agog. Everyone seemed to have caught sight of the creature at one moment or another. Crowds swarmed to the waterfront to see it. The Linnaean Society of New England, meeting in Boston on August 18, quickly organized a committee to gather evidence. Few committees can have been charged with a more fascinating task, and the Bostonians set to work with zest and diligence.

They wrote immediately to the Gloucester justice of the peace, asking him to take sworn depositions from those who saw the "strange sea animal." Their letter stressed that he should question the witnesses as soon as possible after sightings, when their memories were fresh, and should concentrate on people who hadn't yet widely discussed what they had seen. Twenty-five detailed questions, designed to elicit optimum information with minimum verbiage, were set forth. In short, the committee tried to probe thoroughly and intelligently.

Eight depositions were taken—two from ship captains, three from merchants, and one each from a carpenter, a sailor, and the seventeen-year-old son of a prominent citizen. The committee also interviewed three witnesses in Boston, and in Plymouth a Captain Elkanah Finney, who had forthrightly announced a similar sighting two years before.

These cautiously chosen witnesses' stories added up to an account of fitful appearances by the monster during thirteen consecutive days, sometimes for an hour at a time. Sometimes it lazed extended on the surface; sometimes it cavorted like a porpoise; but mostly it pursued and feasted upon schools of herring, which fishermen had been catching in record numbers that year. When it swam with its head high, the head and long neck turned watchfully from side to side, while the body proper rose in a series of humps or bunches, similar to the vertical movement of a caterpillar. It basked for one whole afternoon off Windmill Point, under the scrutiny of two hundred fascinated spectators.

If the "Great American Sea Serpent," as European zoologists jocularly called it, was a mass hallucination, it certainly didn't hypnotize everyone into immobility. On August 20, we are told, an unwarned ship from the fishing banks sailed into the bay, saw the monster, and fled in horror. Traps and nets were set out to capture the creature, but it eluded them gracefully. The revenue cutter came close, veered off, and took on extra guns for defense. A local marksman named Matthew Gaffney fired a bullet at it from a distance of thirty feet, he claimed; someone in another boat said the distance was more like thirty yards. At any rate, the creature submerged and reappeared out of range.

There were a few later reports of sightings in Long Island Sound, and then silence. Two summers later, the leviathan, or one like it, turned up in the waters of Nahant, then a seashore retreat for Boston's elite. Hundreds watched it disport in July and early August. Certain Cabots wrote first-person narratives for Boston newspapers. On August 26 the creature was back at

Gloucester again. There it confronted a U.S. Navy surveying ship, which took optical measurements and calculated its length at a whopping one hundred feet.

Subsequent appearances thereabouts, if any, were not recorded. Backed now by science, naval authority, and the Cabots, the Boston newspapers considered the monster no longer newsworthy. After all, as one editor wrote, "The existence of this fabulous animal is now proven beyond all chance of doubt."

His verdict was too optimistic. Disbelief persisted everywhere but in New England. A story, perhaps apocryphal, relates that a ship's crew sighted a sea serpent and sent word to the captain in his cabin. He refused to go on deck to look at it, explaining later, "Had I said I had seen the sea serpent, I should have been considered a warranted liar my life after."

Perhaps he knew about the ordeal of the captain of H.M.S. *Daedalus* in 1848. Returning from service in the East Indies, that frigate put into Plymouth Harbor on October 4. No sooner had it docked than incredible stories began circulating. The captain and some of the officers and crew were rumored to have seen a monstrous snake in the south Atlantic about three hundred miles off Africa.

The rumor got into the evening papers, and eventually, on October 11, into the London *Times*. Since the sea serpent had become associated with hoaxes and hallucinations, the news reflected discredit on the Royal Navy. Hence, the first sea lord's staff, scanning the *Times* over breakfast, raised its collective eyebrow so abruptly that an official order was dispatched that very morning, instructing Admiral Sir W. H. Gage to find out from the captain of the *Daedalus* what the devil he was up to.

Presumably the admiralty expected a denial of the stories. It must have been taken aback by the prompt reply from Captain Peter M'Quhae of the *Daedalus*. In official nautical terms he affirmed that at 5:00 P.M. on August 6, at a minutely specified latitude and longitude, with the ship heading northeast by north, he and three other officers on the quarterdeck had seen "an enormous serpent, with head and shoulders kept about four feet constantly above the surface of the sea."

They estimated the serpent's visible length at sixty feet, by comparing it with the length of their main topsail yard. It appeared to be fifteen inches thick. It was a dark brownish color. Not only the officers but also the quartermaster, the boatswain's mate, and the helmsman observed the creature for twenty minutes. (The rest of the men were at supper.)

If Captain M'Quhae and his men were conspiring in a hoax, it was pointless and indeed dangerous, for they were lying not only to the public but to the lords of the admiralty, an offense that if discovered would ruin their careers. Had they felt the sighting to be vague or doubtful, they probably would have preferred to keep silent.

Nevertheless, Captain M'Quhae submitted a sketch of the creature with his report. Two other officers of the *Daedalus* sent their own notes to be published. Someone from the ship wrote a long, anonymous letter to the *Times,* rebutting published accusations that those aboard had mistaken a mass of seaweed for a monster.

From these writings we can assemble certain details. The thing had been moving at a speed of "not less than ten miles per hour." It passed within a hundred yards of the ship. At that distance, looking through a telescope, Captain M'Quhae could see it so closely that "had it been a man of my acquaintance I should easily have recognized his features." His impulse was to tack in pursuit, but he realized that the ship could not sail fast enough to overtake it.

Publication of these missives stirred up a rumpus throughout the English-speaking world. Naturalists refused to believe that the huge passerby could be something not sanctioned by the dogmas of their cult; they put forward improbable but mundane theories to account for the episode.

The noisiest spokesman of the antimonster bloc was Professor Sir Richard Owen, curator of the Hunterian Museum and an internationally known anatomist and zoologist. He argued that those who had observed the "sea serpent" were unable to judge what they had seen because they were not trained scientists. What they saw was unquestionably a sea elephant or some other type of large seal, he wrote in a letter to the *Times,* adding charitably, "It is very probable that no one on board ever before beheld a gigantic seal freely swimming."

M'Quhae, a naval officer of long experience, was sure he knew seals and sea elephants when he saw them. His icy response to the *Times* merely reaffirmed that at least sixty feet of the animal had been visible. Inasmuch as the largest recorded specimen of a bull elephant seal is less than twenty-five feet long, Sir Richard's hypothesis didn't seem to fit. The admiralty filed away the documents as one more unsolved mystery of the sea.

A quarter century later, British orthodoxy was again outraged by a Royal Navy captain, this time H. L. Pearson, commander of the royal yacht, the *Osborne.* In an official report to the admiralty, he told of seeing two horrid, ponderous, unidentifiable but not serpentine swimmers off the coast of Sicily. Three other officers aboard confirmed his report. Sir Richard, still in fine fettle, dismissed all four as manifestly incompetent observers. They had been deceived by some optical illusion, he explained.

He also complained that sea serpents were always sighted by sailors, never by scientists. The fact that sailors spend more time at sea than scientists do must have been immaterial, in his view. But in 1905 even Sir Richard's objection ceased to apply—because a sea serpent revealed itself to trained zoologists on a seven-month scientific expedition in the south Atlantic and Indian oceans.

E. G. B. Meade-Waldo and M. J. Nicoll, officials of the London Zoological Society, viewed the monster from the yacht *Valhalla* off Paraíba on the coast of Brazil. The journal of the society boldly published their accounts, which said in part:

A great head and neck rose out of the water. The neck appeared about the thickness of a slight man's body, and from seven to eight feet out of the water; head and neck were all about the same thickness.

The head had a very turtle-like appearance, as had also the eye. I could see the line of the mouth, but we were sailing pretty fast, and quickly drew away from the object, which was going very slowly. It moved its neck from side to side in a peculiar manner. . . .

I feel sure that it was not a reptile that we saw, but a mammal. It is, of course, impossible to be certain of this, but the general appearance of the creature, especially the soft, almost rubber-like fin, gives one this impression.

They had studied it through powerful fieldglasses for ten minutes, at a distance of about a hundred yards. The London Zoological Society was impressed but perhaps embarrassed. It said nothing to the newspapers, and relegated the matter to wherever scientific societies bury inexplicable phenomena.

However, one avidly interested Dutchman took note. He was Dr. Antoon Cornelius Oudemans, director of the zoo at The Hague, who had decided that the great sea serpent was ready for a biographer. He collected and analyzed some six hundred reports, and came forth with a big book, which included details about sightings in 1846 by a Danish Navy captain; in 1872 by two Scottish clerics in a fishing boat, beset near Skye for two days by a vast interloper that passed and repassed, scrutinizing them balefully; in 1883 by a New Zealand captain who saw something resembling a sixty-foot turtle; in 1883 by the skipper of an American whaler, who sent his longboats out to a twenty-foot creature only to see it dive before they reached it; in 1889 by a British captain who saw two monsters together in the Mediterranean; and so on.

A review of the book in *Nature* was not far from abusive. The London *Times* sneered, "A cumbrous and elaborate, albeit quite unconscious, joke." Other critics were less gentle.

Dr. Oudemans had set a complex task for himself.

He had to account for a conglomeration of often contradictory characteristics. There were assertions of sea giants with and without manes, whiskers, humps, fins, tails, and other adjuncts. Estimates of length ranged from ten to a hundred feet. Nevertheless, he assumed that all the grotesque creatures must be substantially alike. He said that they were not serpents nor even reptiles, but a sort of gigantic long-necked seal with small flippers—rather like an ancient plesiosaur, in fact.

The plesiosaur shape would be efficient for a creature that must chase fast-swimming fish. Its fins or flippers would be stabilizers for a long tapering tail. The upcoming generation of oceanographers has exhumed Dr. Oudemans's book and is studying it—for sea monsters keep popping up, and their existence is harder to deny.

There was a sighting—long ago but particularly detailed—by several passengers and crewmen as well as Captain R. J. Cringle, who suffered so much ridicule for his story that he refused to repeat it for thirty-five years afterward. There were several large, fearsome amphibians seen by groups of fishermen in Ireland's deep bays. Off the west coast of Africa, ship passengers spied the head and neck of a monster, and were so convinced of its reality that they elected a committee to make sure their observations were recorded.

Submarines logged a few encounters with massive undersea creatures during the First World War. In the dark depths there could be no certainty whether these were whales, squids, or something else. But Captain F. W. Dean of the Royal Navy filed a statement, duly signed and witnessed, that on May 22, 1917, he and his whole crew observed a sixty-foot creature with a long slender neck maneuvering on the surface about thirty yards away. They watched awhile, then tried to use it for gunnery practice, but it dived like a duck at the first salvo. In response to a pointed query from the admiralty, Captain Dean insisted that the creature definitely could not have been any kind of whale or shark or giant ribbonfish (a species believed to grow as long as twenty feet). These were the substitutes often named by critics as explanations for accounts of monster sightings.

Between 1940 and 1966 at least seventy-five sea monsters were reported. Many naturalists have begun to regard these great unknowns with respect. But the press—and consequently the public—seems to have lost interest. Shore dwellers and ships' passengers no longer mention seeing large strange organisms at sea. Nowadays, if someone observes what he once might have called a sea serpent or monster, he assumes that somehow he is mistaken, or he simply keeps quiet to avoid ridicule.

My opinion is that the ancient fables have become a fascinating fact. Out there in the wastes of sea, giants sometimes slither up out of the darkness onto the surface. Nonviewers may insist on their nonexistence, but I hold with the august *Encyclopaedia Britannica,* which now says of sea monsters:

"When all these and similar possibilities have been explored, there still remain a number of independent and apparently credible stories which are not satisfactorily explained."

8

The Snowman Wants to See You

On December 14, 1974, two Americans and two Sherpa tribesmen left a base camp in northeastern Nepal for a journey into high fastnesses near the vaguely defined borders of Nepal and Sikkim.

They had been in the Himalayas for almost two years, with the Arun Valley Wildlife Expedition. The Arun is one of the world's deepest river valleys. It slashes between the huge masses of Everest and Kanchenjunga, respectively the highest and third highest mountains on earth. Few people have been there, so it remains a primordial paradise for wildlife.

The Americans were Edward W. Cronin, Jr., an eminent zoologist and chief scientist of the Arun expedition; and Dr. Howard Emery, the expedition physician. The purpose of their trip from the base camp was to reconnoiter the unknown shoulders of a mountain called Kongmaa La, and to "investigate the winter conditions of the ecosystem."

Their trip was particularly interesting to me because of my curiosity about legendary man-ape monsters of the Himalayas. I didn't send cameramen into those formidable mountains, nor try to go myself, because I knew of the 1954 and 1958 expeditions that spent months searching at heavy expense without seeing a monster or finding much evidence that one existed. Despite the failures, I suspected that something sinister might be alive up there, so I paid close attention to all available reports from travelers in the region.

Cronin and Emery enjoyed the first few days of their journey, hiking slowly up through the winter-bare forests, breathing deep lungfuls of the diamond air, watching the glories that unfolded at each turn along the slopes. A spicy breeze refreshed them occasionally as they clambered over gigantic hogbacks in hot sunshine.

But later, at a height of nine or ten thousand feet, those breezes from Tibet bit deep. Each pass was colder and higher. Because of the surrounding ridges and the driving clouds, they could seldom glimpse the beauty of the high Himalayas; occasionally an appalling bastion of rock towered ahead of them, like a fragment of a fallen moon, but that was all.

They went over a cruel pass in a storm when driven snow dust filled their eyes and ears and nostrils; they crossed a snowy tableland in cold moonlight, and watched the dawn flare windy-red above stark blue as Mount Makalu took the first sunlight. Their porters had turned back the day before because of the cold, but the four men pressed on, searching for a place to make camp on the great slanting fold of rock connecting to Kongmaa La.

They found a half-acre basin in the ridge at about twelve thousand feet. The flat snowfield was unmarked by prints, so the men thought they were completely alone when they pitched their two light tents there on the afternoon of December 17.

The wind had died and the sun was warm, permitting them to loll in comfort on the ridge and gaze into the enormous pit below. Far down, they could see the Barun River on the north and the Kasuwa River on the south like molten silver under the sun. They ate dinner around an open fire, then crawled into their sleeping bags soon after dark. No wind stirred. No noises broke the silence.

During the night they had a visitor, though they did not know it then.

Something walked up the steep north slope on two oddly shaped flat feet (nine inches long, almost five inches wide). It turned and approached their camp slowly, stalked directly between the tents, and finally strode away down the south slope.

Shortly before sunup Dr. Emery emerged from his tent, and let out a shout when he saw the footprints of the nocturnal wanderer. Seizing cameras, he and Cronin made a full photographic record before the sun touched any of the tracks. Later they made plaster casts.

Most of the footprints were perfectly clear, because the snow was firm and crystalline, smoothed by the winds of previous days. A few of the stranger's tracks merged with their own earlier ones, but elsewhere in the flat area he left some fifteen distinct prints, both left and right feet, showing every detail of spatulate toes, wide round heels, and flat soles.

Emery and Cronin began to follow these prints down the south slope, but there the sun had melted most of the snow, and they lost the track on the bare rock and scrub. They did not dare descend far in their search, because the slope fell away at a perilously steep angle. "Looks as if the creature went straight down toward the forests of the Kasuwa, for some reason," Cronin said. "He must be far stronger than any of us, to stroll down so directly."

Where had he come from?

They backtracked him on the north slope, which was covered with deep snow because it received little sun. Cronin worked his way down beside the tracks for several hundred yards, but found the going slippery because of the snow, and finally gave up when he was forced to cling to rocks with both hands. Yet the visitor evidently had strode up that declivity; his prints seemed to come from over the edge of the earth, up out of the valley far below. He must have been as strong as a gorilla, or stronger, Cronin thought.

Gorillas (largest of the great apes, and man's closest relative) habitually lean on their callused knuckles as they walk or stand. But there were no knuckle marks in the snow. In any case, Africa is the only known habitat of gorillas. The visitor on Kongmaa La presumably was something else.

As a professional biologist with ample experience in the Himalayas, Cronin was sure that the prints were not made by "any known, normal mammal," as he cautiously expressed it. He was not ready to say what had made the footprints.

The two Sherpas had no doubts. At the first glance, they identified the tracks as "yeti footprnts." *Yeti* is a Tibetan word that means "dweller among the high rocks." But the word is now current in English, and our recent dictionaries define it simply as "the Abominable Snowman."

The Snowman, of course, is that mysterious mountain monster for whom so many intrepid Himalayan climbers have searched since 1889, when a British explorer, Major L. A. Waddell, found some sets of unidentifiable, oversized, five-toed footprints in the snows at seventeen thousand feet in Sikkim. Another report came out of Sikkim in 1914, from a British Forestry officer who saw similar footprints.

From time to time since then, tales of a large dark figure moving unseen through groups of sleeping humans have come rolling out of the Himalayas like an avalanche. There have even been a few eyewitness reports.

In 1925 a British photographer and fellow of the Royal Geographical Society, N. A. Tombazi, sighted what he presumed was a yeti near the Zemu Glacier at fifteen thousand feet. He wrote later, "Unquestionably the figure in outline was exactly upright, and stopping occasionally to uproot dwarf rhododendrons. It showed dark against the snow and wore no clothing." Soon afterward a platoon of Russian soldiers was rumored to have shot and killed such a creature in their mountains.

In 1942 a Polish soldier crossing the Himalayan foothills after escaping from a Russian prison camp was confronted by two manlike, hairy giants a hundred yards away, shambling toward him as if they were curious. He outran them. Afterward he estimated that they were about eight feet tall.

In 1948 two Norwegians announced that they had followed a set of yeti tracks, and had overtaken an awesome primate that they boldly tried to lasso. Their attempt failed, and we are spared the details of why or how. The Norwegians came down the mountain with a description of something that walked upright on thick legs, had no tail, and looked more like a human than an ape or bear.

When villagers in the Himalayas are asked about local wildlife, they mention the yeti casually, as one among many: "Yes, we have many wild animals here; there are wolves, bears, yetis, snow leopards, rabbits, and many others."

There is a drawing of an alleged yeti in an eighteenth-century Chinese manuscript on Tibetan wildlife. It shows a stocky manlike creature. His great head tapers toward a furry point on top. His face is hairless and whitish, with deeply sunken red eyes. The rest of his body is covered with short, coarse brownish hair. From massive hunched shoulders, his arms dangle almost to his knees. His size in the drawing is indeterminate.

This picture seems remarkably consistent with descriptions by the various credible eyewitnesses; they all are describing essentially the same creature, and none mentions weird colors, awful fangs, extravagant proportions, or other elaborations to be expected from an imaginative narrator. In short, the descriptions portray a life form that is "exactly what a scientist would expect," at least in Cronin's view as expressed in his report.

But the scientific world, as we have already seen, is cool to reports of uncataloged creatures. "The yeti does not exist," proclaimed one notable scientist who visited the Himalayas. He based this dictum solely on his discovery that the sun could melt known-animal tracks into a semblance of the many photos and plaster casts of alleged yeti tracks.

To him (and to eminent colleagues), this was enough to discredit all the references to yetis in Chinese manuscripts dating back to 200 B.C., as well as a total of forty reports by Westerners since 1832, when the British resident at the Court of Nepal—B. H. Hodgson, an esteemed naturalist of his day—published an account of a yeti seen on a collecting expedition. These witnesses included famous mountaineers like Eric Shipton, Colonel John Hunt, and Sir Edmund Hillary. However detailed and circumstantial their reports, however painstaking their reproductions of the tracks, scientific authorities at home always impugned their reliability: "They may be excellent mountain climbers but how qualified are they to examine spoor or interpret visual sightings? Were they tired or in some way affected by the high altitude? . . . Large unidentifiable footprints could belong to almost any of the wild animals that live in the Himalaya range. At certain gaits, bears place the hind foot partly over the imprint of the forefoot. This makes a very large imprint that looks as if it might be the print of a monster. . . . The Himalayan langur, a monkey with a long tail, often leaves prints that might be mistaken for those of a large unknown animal. . . . Markings thought to be left by the Abominable Snowman could very well have been caused by stones or lumps of snow falling from higher regions and bouncing across the slopes."

Cronin had read such disparagements, and was determined to forestall them this time. (He probably did not know that his case would be strengthened because Peter Byrne, an American explorer, had found two sets of yeti tracks in the mountains above this same Arun Valley in 1957.) By matching his own footprints made on the night of December 17 with those he made the next morning, he proved to his own satisfaction that all prints near the camp had remained unaltered by any night wind or early-morning sunshine.

He knew all about bear tracks, langur tracks, and other prints nominated as "explanations" for yeti tracks. He wrote in his report:

> During the expedition we devoted special efforts to examining all large mammal prints made in snow.
> We noted possible variations produced by different snow conditions, terrain, and activities of the animal (i.e., running, walking, etc.); a photographic record was made. We feel we can eliminate any possibility that the prints are referable to a local animal. . . .

Based on this experience, I believe there is a creature alive today in the Himalayas which is creating a valid zoological mystery. . . . The evidence points to a new form of bipedal primate.

Or perhaps a very old form, he thought.

Paleontologists deduce from fossils that nine million years ago a breed of mighty apes, which they have christened *Gigantopithecus,* roamed widely in southern Asia. These hulking creatures flourished for at least eight and a half million years—so eventually they were contemporaries of man's ancestor, *Homo erectus.*

Suppose the huge apes came in contact with evolving man in India or thereabouts. The two species probably would have competed. A basic principle of population biology, the competitive-exclusion principle, lays down the rule that whenever two similar forms of life arise in the same area, one will flee or become extinct as it loses the competition for food and other necessities.

A half-million years ago, man had already learned about fire. He had learned to make tools of stone, bone, and wood. Thus his rivals, the giant apes, would have been at a fatal disadvantage. Perhaps they died out. Paleontologists think so, because their fossils have not been found in later strata. But what if *Gigantopithecus* simply moved out of man's way? What if he wandered up into the Himalayas? Might he not survive there, right up to the present?

In Africa, gorillas are known to inhabit mountains as high as thirteen thousand feet. Cronin could visualize *Gigantopithecus* doing equally well in the Himalayas. "There is no zoological, paleontological, or ecological reason to suppose that an unknown anthropoid does not exist in the Himalayas," he told his colleagues firmly.

But he did not assert that this anthropoid—the theoretical Snowman—dwelt permanently in the harsh cloudlands of perpetual snow. Cronin surmised that when a yeti is in the snows it is en route over a snowy pass from one valley to the next. In the Himalayas— the highest mountain range in the world—gaps and ridges are the only possible paths for travel between valleys.

Where the yeti really lives, Cronin now thinks, is in the tangled forests at the middle-altitude level of the Himalayas. These zones abound with lush plants that offer food for many species of large mammals. Monstrous primates might thrive there—never seen by man, who seldom enters the dense growths of rhododendron, fir, alder, beech, bamboo, and fern.

The wooded areas look deceptively small on a two-dimensional map. But folded within them are huge patches of steep country. The rare human who does venture into these wooded areas must keep to the ridges and stream beds, because the undergrowth is too thick to penetrate. Cronin had gone in, but had to cut his way with a machete.

"Only a creature born in and adapted to these conditions could travel through the vegetation with ease," he reported. "It would have been possible for a large mammal to hide within fifty yards of me and remain unnoticed."

Another clue that suggests *Gigantopithecus* as ancestor of the yeti is the "pointed head" mentioned so often by those who have seen monsters in the Himalayas. Fragments of fossilized bones identified with *Gigantopithecus* indicate that it had a big jaw and bulging jaw muscles. "In apes, this is often associated with a tall sagittal crest . . . as an attachment point for these muscles," Cronin wrote, "and would exactly duplicate the pointed head."

If the yeti did evolve from the giant ape of nine million years ago, he wouldn't necessarily resemble the gorillas known to today's naturalists. Dian Fossey, an American scientist who spent three years living among wild mountain gorillas in their age-old highland haunts, said, "The gorilla is one of the most maligned animals in the world. . . . Beneath his fierce appearance lies a shy and gentle nature."

Even after thousands of hours of close observation, Ms. Fossey and other experts on gorilla behavior are perplexed by certain mysteries about the species. They cannot say, for example, what becomes of dead gorillas.

Ms. Fossey saw one matriarchal female, whom she called Koko, disappear into the deep woods with a mate known as Rafiki, a wise old silverback. When Rafiki returned alone two days later, Ms. Fossey immediately backtracked his trail. "It showed that Koko had shared night nests with Rafiki, and then it seemed as if the earth had literally swallowed her up," the zoologist reported. "What happened to the body of Koko I shall probably never know."

No remains of anything like a yeti have ever been found. This is another reason why skeptics insist that the yeti does not exist. However, big-game hunters in Africa have written that they have never heard of anybody coming upon a dead elephant. Insects, carrion scavengers, and fast-growing vegetation could conceivably obliterate all clues to anything that dies in a jungle. It is harder to imagine how monsters dying in the high snows would vanish. This adds weight to Cronin's theory that the Snowman lives down in the valleys rather than up among the peaks.

Gorillas are monstrous enough, sometimes weighing four hundred pounds or more, with eight-foot arm spans. But they are seldom more than six feet tall, whereas yetis are usually described as taller than men. Some yeti footprints are twelve or thirteen inches long and as wide as seven inches, with the heel nearly as broad as the forepart. Such feet might fit a truly gigantic primate. (Cronin decided that the prints he found, of smaller dimensions, were probably made by an abnormally small yeti—perhaps a youngster—weighing only about 165 pounds.)

The shy Snowman, so stealthy that he is almost never seen, might be considered less abominable than inquisitive. If so, he is somewhat like the gorilla in this respect. Gorillas are nervous and watchful when in the vicinity of humans—although Ms. Fossey found it easy to make friends with them after she had won their confidence, because their natural curiosity overcame their timidity.

Gorillas have never been seen eating meat in the wild, unlike their kin the chimpanzees, which sometimes kill and devour baboons, monkeys, and bush pigs. On the other hand, a gorilla's immense strength makes him dangerous. There are recorded cases of gorillas attacking humans who provoked them. If the Snowman is indeed bigger and stronger than the gorilla, he may be proportionately more terrible when aroused.

In 1975 a Nepalese police officer reported a statement made by a mountain girl: "Lhakpa said she got a good look at the beast as it ripped the throat of her only cow and slaughtered her yaks by smashing their heads with its huge fists. . . . I'm convinced the girl saw a yeti. No other beast I know of could have mutilated her animals that way."

In Bhutan (the inaccessible little protectorate of India in the eastern Himalayas next to Tibet and Sikkim) it is said that yaks are sometimes found mangled, with their necks snapped like celery stalks. Villagers attribute these killings to yetis, and live in dread of them.

On the other hand, Tenzing Norgay, Sikkim's most famous Sherpa mountaineer, says that a yeti once crawled on top of a yak herder's hut at night and lazed there, enjoying the warmth from a fire in the hut, until the frightened shepherd piled yak dung on the fire and drove the monster away with smoke.

Nancy Wilson Ross, who has traveled widely in the Far East as an official representative of the Asia Society of New York, was invited to a royal wedding at Gangtok, the capital of Sikkim, in March 1963. She wrote an account of her visit for *Horizon,* in which she quoted Princess Pema Tsedeun, one of the maharaja's daughters, as saying:

"Of course the yeti feeds on human beings too. That's why he arouses such fear and why he has been given such filthy, unclean names. No, the Snowman is certainly not a myth. Lamas in lonely monasteries, and Sherpa climbers, have given quite exact descriptions."

Implying that there might be something supernatural and demonic about the yetis, the princess added that she had sensed the unseen presence of one while on a journey with porters through lonely mountains. "At evening we heard it, far off like a high wind—only it wasn't a wind," she told Ms. Ross. The porters fell flat in terror, arms over their heads. She remained upright, as a princess should, but closed her eyes and prayed. Soon she heard the Snowman pass by. "Trees were falling, but there was no real wind. It was very different altogether. It was just a—tremendous, overwhelming presence."

In Gangtok there is a story that a yeti once carried off a palace servant. A party of expert climbers went to the rescue. They saw giant footprints ascending Kanchenjunga and followed them onto a ledge, where they saw the Snowman, curiously watching his captive scrabble in the ice. The poor man was unharmed but mad, according to this tale, and never regained his sanity.

There is no proven case of a yeti carrying off a human, but there have been unexplained disappearances in the cold wastes of the upper Himalayas.

In 1895 a British expedition under Albert Frederick Mummery, the most successful mountaineer of his generation, vanished on a slope of Nanga Parbat. No trace was ever found.

In 1924 two other legendary British explorers, George H. Leigh-Mallory and Andrew Irvine, climbed up into a mist six hundred feet from Everest's summit. When it became apparent that they were missing, Sherpas went to search, but found only their empty tents. Years later a rusted ice ax belonging to one of the two men was found at about twenty-eight thousand feet—a thousand feet below the peak. This only deepened the mystery. "The fate of Mallory and Irvine has haunted mountaineers since," said a *Life* article.

A 1934 expedition lost four men.

Four Austrian women vanished in 1959 while ascending Cho Oyu in Nepal.

Likely explanations for such disappearances could be avalanches, crevasses, and shrieking storms that can blow a climber off a mountain wall. But the horrid possibility—of intervention by a yeti—cannot be ruled out altogether.

Sikkim is a kingdom where belief in unseen forces is

strong. There are impressive reasons for this. Ms. Ross tells of a single tree left untrimmed and undecorated in the garden where a royal wedding reception was to be held. She asked about this conspicuous neglect, and was told that the tree was never touched because it was inhabited by a spirit who "did not take kindly to being disturbed." Later, she related, a Western-educated guest from Bhutan undertook to dispel this superstition by giving the tree a hearty kick. The next morning his whole leg and foot were painfully swollen, and remained so for several days.

Sikkim's maharaja, Sir Tashi Namgyal, was said to be a wizard. There were three reliably documented examples of his alleged power to control the weather on special occasions. In 1956, in honor of a state visit by Tibet's Dalai Lama, Sir Tashi reportedly rolled back the clouds that almost always hide Kanchenjunga. Two years later, when Nehru paid a visit, Sir Tashi escorted him to the top of the Natu La Pass, which was shrouded in a cold drizzle as usual. There the sky suddenly cleared for half an hour, affording Nehru a good view of Red Chinese encroachments in Tibet. Finally, in 1963, while Ms. Ross herself was there, Sir Tashi was credited with keeping the weather warm and sunny for his two hundred wedding guests. Immediately before and after the week of festivities, the Gangtok weather was considered normal for the season: chilly and rainy, with heavy hailstorms.

Ms. Ross particularly wanted to know about the Abominable Snowman. She had promised William O. Douglas of the U.S. Supreme Court that she would try to continue a conversation he had had with Sir Tashi years earlier. Douglas had asked if the maharaja had ever seen the mythical Himalayan creature. "Oh, yes, regularly," Sir Tashi replied, and when his startled guest inquired where, the old sovereign answered, as mildly as if mentioning a family croquet game, "Right on the palace lawn."

An interruption prevented Douglas from pursuing the subject. Ms. Ross hoped to find out just what His Highness had meant. During a private conversation,

she conveyed the justice's respectful greetings, and
went on to say that Mr. Douglas had suggested she in-
quire about the Snowman.

"Oh, yes, to be sure, I still see the yeti," Sir Tashi
replied in a matter-of-fact tone. "He visits me on the
twenty-ninth of every month." Sir Tashi showed her a
vivid painting he had done himself and kept in his private studio. It showed a coal-black demon carrying a
naked woman off toward distant snowcapped peaks.
This was the yeti, he indicated.

Somewhat confused, Ms. Ross nevertheless managed
to keep Sir Tashi talking about his monthly visitor, and
was told that the demon came in different disguises—
"sometime golden armor"—and was seen by nobody
else except two lamas.

Sir Tashi, a good Buddhist, felt that the fierce wraith
was as entitled to compassion and brotherly concern
as were all the other blind and unblind "intelligences"
of nature. Therefore, on occasions when the Snowman
tweaked him or shoved him, Sir Tashi merely remon-
strated mildly. "I say, 'Come, come now, that's enough
of that.' Then he leaves."

Ms. Ross, and those to whom she related the conversation, have wondered whether His Highness was
quietly spoofing her. The question cannot be answered,
for he died in November 1963. Gangtok people say
he was the last of the royal wizards of the Himalayan
world.

However that may be, it is certain that belief in
fierce ghosts persists around Kanchenjunga. Whether
the ghosts are different from the Snowman, or identical
with him, is not for Westerners to say. It would not be
the first time that a natural monster has frozen the
blood of beholders with fear of a supernatural substi-
tute.

9

America's Longest Hide-and-Seek Game

As I watched the hulking, brownish figure stride across the movie screen, I felt an odd sensation of displacement—as if I might be somewhere else.

I knew, in some part of my mind, that if I just pulled my eyes away, I could snap back to where I really was, in an Oregon town. But the jerky, hairy image on the screen almost hypnotized me for a few seconds: my surroundings didn't exist; the darkened room had emptied of people; the streets outside were gone. I was far back in a time before the memory of man, alone with the giant ghost.

Never slackening its long swift strides, it glanced over its shoulder, seemingly straight at me. Then it looked ahead again, and soon was gone.

In the instant when our eyes met, I felt an almost electrical shock of recognition. Maybe I had a strange kinship with the ugly creature. The stare of those dark eyes was not hateful, nor fearful, nor even recognizing. The eyes were set deep, and spaced like a human's, yet the broad-nosed face was masked with hair, and looked anthropoid.

The screen went blank. I sat in a kind of trance for what seemed a long time, but it may have been only a heartbeat or two.

Sometimes I have a fourth-dimensional sensitivity to an ancient artifact or to a place drowned in time. Never before had a strip of color film from a hand-held camera given me the sensation, but this one definitely did.

There were flashes of forgotten lives, of antediluvian creatures arising out of ancestral dreams. I saw and felt—almost lived—a jumble of scenes from unknown places.

A night of glittering cold starlight. Above me, slopes of forest-covered hills rising in silent mystery. Distant sky red with the glow of a volcano. The black mouth of a cave at my back. The ancient Friend, fire, beside me. Out yonder, huge dreadful enemies who walked by night.

No men out there. We men were still new hereabouts.

We had been coming slowly along the rivers, generation after generation, from one squatting place to another. Vaguely I knew that our tribe had walked on dry land from far away in the northwest, across strange bridges and down green corridors out of a distant place that would be called Asia someday, through another place to be called Alaska, into this region of easier hunting and less ice.

Now I stood waiting. Soon the Terror would come calling.

I had smelled his stink, heard his footsteps crunching swiftly up the hillside from the brook.

At last he edged into the yellow circle of firelight, and stood swaying: a terrible long-armed giant, chest and arms dark with thick hair. I saw that my head would be as high as his great hunched shoulders.

The Terror was lord of the rocks and caves, just as the grizzly bear was lord of the thick woods below. None preyed on him, none gave him battle. Even the mammoth shunned his stamping places. But he could be taught to keep away.

This one seemed uncertain. He sniffed the acrid scent of wood smoke, peered at the Friend's jumping flames. I shook my mane of hair and howled a warning. He did not move. I knew he had never seen the Friend before, else he would not be so close.

He started for me with a high squalling yell, but I was ready, my hand on a stout stick in the fire. It was flaming as I poked it up at his awful face. It hit a hairy cheek with a burst of sparks. He stumbled back, slapping and rubbing at the sparks. I brandished the blazing cudgel, and he shrieked again and stalked away. I knew he would never return when the Friend was with me.

Flashes of other times came. There was a noonday sun and I was away from my squatting place. I lay guzzling at a stream. In its rush I heard nothing else. Suddenly the Terror towered over me, gigantic against the blue. He seldom came out by day and I was horribly surprised. I rolled, scrambled to my feet and ran, but in a few giant strides he caught me, and there was no more of that.

Another time: late afternoon, and I, in a tree, frightened. I had smelled the faint, foul reek of the Terror somewhere near. The ground was melting to ominous quiet purple pools, shadows were browning the tree trunks; they climbed on branches and watched me. Then the owl, flitting silently, came ghostly through the shades. The world darkened until leaves and twigs against the sky were black, and the ground was hidden. In those days men were never alone in the dark, save for such rare accidents as this. Age after age we had learned the lesson of its perils.

Now something was coming. Something very tall, with thick hair. Something swinging along with soft swift strides. I knew him from other times: the Terror.

A stir in the thicket. Then vigorous movement. There was a snap. Reeds crashed heavily, once, twice, then there was only a measured swishing. Had the Terror scented me?

Yes. From below I heard a snuffling growl. He looked upward, and began to rock the tree. He must have seen me: the Terror sees well at night.

He might shake me down, or even pull the tree down with his terrible strength, but I had a chance, for I had brought a rock up the tree with me. I dropped it straight down. I heard a deadly thunk, and the tree stopped rocking. There came a deep, resonant, nasal groan. The Terror lurched away into the thicket. He would not hunt us again.

Another time: I myself was a giant, perplexed at an invasion of strange small creatures that moved on only two feet, like me. These new creatures were slow and weak. They were monkey-shaped, but sparsely hairy like young pigs. Monkey and young pig, I thought. It might be good eating. I caught and crunched one. But I had never seen the yellow thing that flickered, and the black shapes leaping behind it. I was curious.

The first time, I saw the bright thing grow bigger and become a deep orange, while up and down the gorge things that had been unseen came clear, and I wondered if the dawn was coming in the wrong place. These intrusions stirred me with a sense of strange new happenings. I went close. But the flaring brightness hurt me. I went away.

Next time I stood watching for a very long time. At last the yellow and orange got small, then glimmered. Its thick billowing mist above straightened into one wavering gray line. The two-legged things were inside the cave—a place where I myself liked to sleep when days were hot and glary.

Pig and monkey, I remembered. Eat. I began to climb.

The new creatures ran and poked quickly at the place where the yellow leaper had been, but it was only grayness. I seized a creature that tried to scamper away, and began to tear it. The other creatures were jumping around instead of running off.

I noticed that they swung things I had never seen before. Big stones at one end. One broke into my side, and hot blood gushed over my hand. I roared with surprise and anger. Then I glimpsed another stone knob coming at my eyes, and that was all.

A different half instant: I was squatting somewhere. In front was a steady rustling, a splash, and the reeds swayed wider and wider apart. Then they broke open, cleft from root to tips. My blood seemed to freeze as I looked up at the thing that came out of the reeds.

Hair-covered, beetle-browed, flat-nosed, ears with no lobes and little pointed tips, terrible thick arms reaching out such a long way at me.

"Do you think the film was genuine or hoked?" someone asked.

The lights were on and my television-production crew stood around. I was in The Dalles, Oregon, on the track of another monster—this time a monster that I might know subliminally.

I was sure it hadn't been a man in a fur suit. The legs were too stumpy for a man, the arms too long, the body too broad and chesty. And those long easy strides —each time it took a step it went maybe four feet.

To verify that the film footage was genuine, I decided to get in touch with Dr. John Napier of the University of London, who had studied the film frame by frame. He had at one time been the Smithsonian Institution's expert on primates. I also wanted to contact Dr. Grover Krantz at Washington State University, a physical anthropologist who had done a buildup from plaster casts of the footprints.

In the meantime, I wanted to take a look at the file, to ascertain the facts behind the footage.

The file showed that the film had been shot along the mostly dry bed of a tiny stream called Bluff Creek, near California's far northwestern corner. Large naked manlike footprints had been found before in that wild area. Lured by hopes of capturing at least on film an authentic monster unknown to science, two venturesome men had gone on horseback through forests to the Bluff Creek area.

They were Roger Patterson, a rodeo rider from Tampico, Washington, and his pal from nearby Union Gap, a horse breeder and cattleman named Bob Gimlin. For four years, off and on, the pair had been prospecting through every region where these giant tracks had been reported—in the massive mountains of British Columbia, Washington, Oregon, and northernmost California. They kept a camera ready in a saddlebag.

On Friday, October 20, 1967, they camped on the

west bank of Bluff Creek just above where Notice Creek joined it. Patterson spent the morning photographing scenery and wildlife, as part of a general film he planned on the search for the furtive man-monsters of the Pacific Range. About one-fifteen that afternoon the two men were riding north in the bed of the creek, watching for footprints. Their horses made little or no noise on the soft gray sand.

Ahead was a jumble of uprooted trees, washed out and piled up by a flood of years before. The pile was probably fifteen feet high. It stretched across the stream bed, hiding their approach from anything behind it.

They came around the logjam together and found a great something-or-other squatting on the bank of the watercourse. It immediately stood up and walked away.

The horses panicked and reared. Gimlin slid off and managed to hold his horse. Patterson's horse fell over sideways, pinning him. In a frenzy of haste he wrestled free, pulled out the camera, and ran after the huge walker.

The creature was crossing the stream. Patterson aimed the camera from about a hundred feet away, and kept a finger pressed on the trigger until his remaining twenty-eight feet of film ran out. Then the camera was empty, the man-thing was gone, and it was all over.

The horses had bolted. The men knew they must retrieve them before doing anything else. They hiked south a mile and found the horses grazing. Then they galloped back to the scene, tied the horses, and began trying to track what they had seen.

They could not. Its trail led up across bare rocks. After searching a long time they went back to the photo site and made plaster casts of the creature's footprints in the sand. These were about half again as large as a human foot. Then they packed up, rode to their horse-carrier truck, and drove to the town where they sent the film by registered airmail to Yakima for processing. By Saturday night it was the talk of Yakima.

No one who watched the footage could find any indication of trickery. But many who didn't see it were derisive. They surmised that Gimlin and Patterson took a secret partner along, a big man who zipped himself into some craftily sewn fur suit and strode along the creek to be photographed.

Another theory held that the supposed third man was in cahoots with only Patterson, and the two of them were bamboozling Gimlin. The accomplice could have been hiding, ready to show himself for the few seconds when the horses were panicked. "It happened too fast for Gimlin to wise up," some said knowingly.

The site of the alleged encounter came under intense scrutiny. Maps showed, surprisingly, that it was within clear view of two roads. One ran along Bluff Creek's east side, close to the stream bed and at places almost in it. It was a dirt road cut by a tractor in a log-removal program. Any four-wheel-drive vehicle could negotiate it. The other road also paralleled the creek, but was cut into the bank about a thousand feet above. Originally a logging road, it had been converted to an all-weather road with a bitumen surface. From this road any driver could see the whole area where Patterson shot the film.

Several groups bent on exposing fraud—or on finding proof of a true monster—drove the paved road and made the arduous scramble down the bluff to the creek. There they found clear marks of the action Gimlin and Patterson had described: horses' hooves and the mark of a fall, sets of boot prints matching the two men's boots, and a set of big naked tracks matching the plaster casts. No tracks of any other person were found. It was hard to see how the encounter could have been rigged.

Talk turned to the possibility that Gimlin and Patterson had molded fake bare feet and pressed them into the sand. The strides were about forty-two inches long. Their depth led to weight estimates ranging from 350 to 800 pounds, so if Gimlin and Patterson had used artificial feet, they had to press down with some tremendous weights.

If the creature was genuine, how tall was it? Serious monster seekers tried to find out by taking photos of human models, for comparison with Patterson's pictures, at the place where Patterson shot, matching the background as perfectly as possible. They measured trees, stumps, rocks, and everything else visible behind the monster in the film. Still, they couldn't be sure just where Patterson was when he aimed his camera; he was moving as he shot the film. Anyway, the pictures seemed to put the creature's height between six feet and six-six.

I rummaged back through what I knew of legendary human giants.

The Bible described Goliath as "six cubits and a span" (I Samuel 17:4). Cubits and spans were variable, but they would make Goliath at least nine feet nine inches tall. Maybe someone exaggerated.

Charlemagne (whose name meant "Big Charles") was six feet four, as indicated by his skeleton—unimpressive now, but a good twelve inches above most men of his time.

But there have been genuine giants within the last century. In 1880, Londoners measured a Norwegian named Brusted at an even eight feet, and found a Chinese named Ching two inches taller. Benjamin Holmes, who died in Northumberland in 1892, was seven-six.

I once saw an eight-foot-six-inch skeleton in a Dublin college museum. London's College of Surgeons still exhibits the eight-four skeleton of Charles Byrne, who died in 1783. As many as twenty-two other individuals who lived in the eighteenth century or later are recorded in reference books as being at least seven and a half feet tall.

Was there some aberrant gene, I wondered, that produced an occasional enormous human?

In Old Testament times there may have been tribes or even kingdoms of giant-sized people. Bashan's King Og, who was said to sleep on an iron bed of startling size, "remained of the remnant of giants," according to Deuteronomy 3:11, and that same chapter called Bashan "the land of giants." Numbers 13:22 and 33 mention "the giants, the sons of Anak," who seem to have been a tribe on the banks of the Jordan. The Rephaim were described as a race of giants eight different times in Genesis, Deuteronomy, and Joshua.

No scientist used to take such biblical big talk literally—until archaeologists dug up the famous "great stone graves," or dolmens, in the Jordan country. One was precisely at the old site of Rabbath, where Deuteronomy said King Og's bedstead lay. "Nine cubits was the length thereof, and four cubits the breadth," it specified in 3:11. The grave contained a "bed" of basalt, a very hard gray-black stone that could be taken for iron. It was roughly the length and breadth specified in the Bible.

But this turned out to be less extraordinary than it seemed. Huge stone graves proved fairly common in Palestine; more than a thousand have been opened in the coarse grass of the highlands. Similar graves, which local peasants have called "giants' beds" since time immemorial, are now authenticated archaeological relics in northern Germany, Denmark, England, and northwestern France. More recently, graves just as large have come to light in India and eastern Asia.

These clues to supernormal-size men reminded me of the *Gigantopithecus* apes of millions of years ago, which I mentioned in the last chapter. These huge apes, and mankind, were divergent strains evolving from a common ancestor somewhere in the aeons after dinosaurs vanished. Could there have been intermingling of the strains up to comparatively recent times, say our Stone Age?

At any rate, I thought, the continued survival of a hidden breed of huge hominids or anthropoids might be as possible in the Pacific Northwest as in the Himalayas. And if they stood seven feet, this wouldn't be phenomenal, even though science has no fossils of apes or gorillas nearly that tall. The record of the rocks is far from complete, as we have seen. Science would never have accepted the possibility of eight-foot men, were it not for their skeletons and graves.

Because of the lack of bones or fossils, scientists still shrug at Indian legends of the Sasquatch ("hairy men") who supposedly haunt some American mountain ranges. These are said to be descendants of aboriginal giants whom the Indians "almost killed off" in battle many generations ago.

White settlers in the Pacific Northwest built up their own legend of Bigfoot, a seldom-seen biped that sometimes left tracks of five-toed feet in lonely forest glades. The tracks were like a human's but much bigger—occasionally as long as seventeen inches, as wide as five. Bigfoot seemed to take commensurately long strides, up to fifty-six inches.

The Sasquatch and Bigfoot tales were what pulled me to The Dalles, in the heart of "Bigfoot country" on the Columbia River. In that town is the Bigfoot Information Center, presided over by Peter Byrne, whom I knew by repute.

Byrne was a wartime Royal Air Force pilot who later made a name in Nepal as an explorer, big-game hunter, and tracker. He often guided sportsmen on tiger hunts. But when he realized that the tiger was on the verge of extinction he changed to hunting with cameras instead of guns; he established Asia's first tiger sanctuary, and helped found the International Wildlife Conservation Society.

He prowled the Himalayas on four expeditions in search of the Snowman, and photographed its footprints. When he studied yeti lore he saw the possibility that *Gigantopithecus* had not only fled into the Himalayas but had also wandered across the Bering Strait when it was dry land, and then had spread through American mountains—perhaps evolving into something bigger than their Asian cousins.

If any of these wild ape-men still survived, he yearned to find them. Tom Slick, a Texas oil millionaire and monster buff who had subsidized Byrne's last two yeti hunts, offered to back him in seeking Bigfoot. So Byrne went to Oregon in 1960. He and Slick found twelve sets of Bigfoot prints that year. Not a glimpse did they get, however, of Bigfoot.

Then Slick died in an air crash. Byrne went back to Nepal, but the Bigfoot bug was in his blood. In 1970 he returned to resume the search, this time pumping

$100,000 of his own money into it. In 1972 he devised a way to make the quest almost self-supporting.

He put a fifty-five-foot mobile home on a permanent site at West Sixth Street in The Dalles, and mounted a collection of exhibits—photos and casts of the huge tracks, maps that pinpointed tracks and ninety-four "credible sightings," brochures that told details about them, and newspaper and magazine features. By charging admission to this exhibition hall, Byrne kept enough cash flowing in to pay most of his search and investigation expenses.

His Bigfoot Information Center began to receive letters, phone calls, and personal visits from people who said they had seen a giant or its tracks. Byrne gave everyone careful hearings, kept names confidential whenever asked to do so, and pursued every lead that sounded promising.

So he was a man worth meeting.

After watching the Patterson-Gimlin footage (the only pictures Byrne considered worth seeing) my next logical step was to interview Byrne.

At fifty, he was, I thought, the picturesque prototype of a rugged adventurer: tall and lean, handsome in an urbane patrician style, frosting at the temples. Perhaps you saw, or will see, our interview in my NBC television series.

"What makes you keep searching for Bigfoot?" was my first question.

He said in his soft Irish brogue (he comes from a family of Dublin gentry), "I've been asked that many times. I'm the only man who has made a profession of this extraordinary search. For most of my life I've been a hunter, professionally and emotionally—and for a hunter this is perhaps the ultimate hunt. The quarry is the rarest of all big game—a possibly highly intelligent, highly mobile, partially nocturnal creature with a habitat of a hundred thousand square miles in some of the most difficult country in the world."

"How far are we from finding this thing?"

Sadness tinged his smile. "It has eluded me now for six years. We make progress, but it's very slow. If we had proper funding I think we could find one within two years. But we're not doing the kind of research we should, through lack of support. It may take many years.

"But I'm not discouraged. Every time my phone rings there's the thrill of knowing this call could lead to the quarry. Every time we race to the scene of a new sighting, we know we may find one of the giant primates around the bend."

He recalled that the chase had led him more than 150,000 miles at the wheel of his trusty International Scout. He had roped his way up cliffs, followed bloodhounds through snowstorms, and gotten himself shipwrecked and stranded for eight days in the British Columbian straits. Night-after night he still crouched in high-altitude lookout posts, often in subzero cold, peering through a snooperscope on loan from the army.

It was obvious that he was driven by almost obsessive determination to confront this hairy enigma, even if it took a lifetime—almost like Ahab and the white whale. I said, "Hunters are itching to bring back a dead Bigfoot. Still they've never gotten a shot at one. Could pranksters be trundling through the trees from time to time, making imitation tracks and posing as Bigfoot? Could some sightings be hallucinations, or just plain lies?"

His dark eyebrows knotted at the mention of hunters. "Shooting one of these creatures would be criminal. There aren't many alive—maybe as few as two hundred. They're nearly human, or anyhow less vicious than our kind. In all our investigations there's no report of aggression. Think of all the fisherman, hikers, snowmobilers, and young children who go into these dense forests. If Bigfoot were dangerous I think there would be attacks, abductions, disappearances—and there is no such record during the past two centuries. So we look on them as benign, inoffensive creatures. We hope to get an executive order to protect them from hunters.

"As for pranksters," he went on more quietly, "you should ask Dr. Napier how difficult it would be to fake footprints as convincing as some we've seen. Newspapers sometimes make it sound as if only a single footprint were found, but the more typical discovery is a long set of tracks. Where the ground is soft, prints are sometimes detailed enough for anatomists to reconstruct the whole foot that made the print. . . . Oh, there've been fake films, fake tracks. They're troublesome to us because we have to spend time examining them. The motive mainly is money. People can make money selling this stuff. When we find it we expose it. This is one reason there hasn't been much faking lately.

"Another reason is that the back country is bristling with hunters who want a shot at Bigfoot. Pretending to be the creature could easily get a person killed. Would anyone travel thousands of miles for the doubtful gratification of showing himself for a few seconds to some hard-working and rather disinterested woodman? Would a hoaxer find reward in sitting on the edge of a freezing mountain road in the wilds, waiting for someone to come along and have a quick look at him?"

Byrne's files listed five sightings worth checking in 1971, three in 1972, and four each in 1973, '74, and '75. Altogether he has compiled details of ninety-four reported sightings that seem believable. As for tracks, the files bulge with listings, including one trail of three thousand prints that Byrne photographed in the dust of a lonely logging road in the Cascade Range.

People were seeking the Northwest's elusive giants long before Byrne's time. The hunt may have started when Leif Ericson and his crew made their first landing in the New World; according to the Norse sagas, they encountered creatures described as "horribly ugly, hairy, swarthy, with great black eyes." Maybe the Norsemen were talking about Indians. But the word *hairy* in their accounts is curious. The voyagers were hairy themselves—big men with matted hair and beards. Why were they struck by the hairiness of the beings they saw? Perhaps it was because these creatures were much hairier than the Norsemen themselves, or perhaps even covered with hair, as Bigfoot and Sasquatch seem to be.

We'll never know for sure. Nor will we know what

kernels of truth there are, if any, in the old tales of
"big people in the mountains" among the Nootka and
Salish tribes of Canada, the Athapaskans of Washington and Oregon, the Celilo tribe that once lived along
the Columbia River, and the Hoopas and Hokans of
northern California. These tribes believed in mountain
monsters, feared them, and stayed away from their
reputed haunts.

An 1840 letter from Elkanah Walker, a missionary
to the Nez Percés and Flatheads in upper Washington,
mentions casually:

> They believe in the existence of a race of giants
> which inhabit a certain mountain off to the west of
> us, [and] hunt and work in the night. . . .
> The account will in some measure correspond with
> the Bible account of this race of beings. They say
> their track is about a foot and a half long. They will
> carry two or three beams upon their back at once.
> If people are awake they always know when they
> are coming near, by their strong smell, which is most
> intolerable.

This missionary's allusion to giants in the mountains
wasn't the first by a white man. Thirty years earlier, a
fur trader named David Thompson wrote in his diary
that he found huge footprints in the Rocky Mountains
at the place where Jasper is now. The prints were eight
inches wide, fourteen inches long. He thought they
might be paw prints of a colossal bear, but they lacked
the characteristic claw marks.

Indian guides told him the prints were those of a
two-footed mammoth (the word was Thompson's, but
it is still used by some Indians to describe the Sasquatch). He urged his guides to follow the tracks, but
they refused.

Walker's and Thompson's accounts were found in
their private papers. The oldest known published account of an American equivalent of the Abominable
Snowman appeared in an 1886 pamphlet about Siski-
you County, California:

I do not remember to have seen any reference to the "Wild Man" which haunts this part of the country, so I shall allude to him briefly. Not a great while since, Mr. Jack Dover, one of our most trustworthy citizens, while hunting saw an object standing one hundred and fifty yards from him picking berries or tender shoots from the bushes. The thing was gigantic, about seven feet high.

Mr. Dover could not see its footprints as it walked on hard soil. He aimed his gun several times, but because it was so human would not shoot. . . . A number of people have seen it and agree in their descriptions, except some make it taller than others.

As the Pacific Northwest valleys began to fill with towns, legends of Bigfoot and Sasquatch faded into obscurity. There were occasional rumors of big and hairy phantoms somewhere up near the timberline, but townspeople paid little attention.

In 1958, however, a report came down that compelled attention. A whole road crew had seen giant footprints around their camp in the remote mountains of Humboldt County in northern California. To prove it, they made casts of some of the prints and brought them out to a newspaper editor in Eureka. He front-paged the story, with a photo of the monstrous plaster feet. The story was picked up by news wire services and national magazines. It emboldened a number of old settlers to say that they too had seen such footprints, or a hairy giant itself, at some time in past decades, but hadn't said so for fear of ridicule.

From then on, Bigfoot reports popped up every year. Most of the sightings and trackings clustered along the spines of the coast ranges and the Cascade Range. I had spent some time wandering through those mountains. I knew of vast areas where there are no scars of forest-fire devastation, no curling smoke from campfires, no honks of car horns, no whistles of trains. No litterbugs have been there. Nobody is there at all. As far as we know, nobody has *ever* been in some of the canyons.

But Bigfoot isn't invariably so remote. "Sometimes there are sightings in areas that have always been wilderness but are now being opened up," a hunter named Ed McClarney told me. "People get very fleeting glances, or see footprints."

I browsed through reports in the information center. In 1959 a startled deputy sheriff stood transfixed as a towering hairy thing approached through trees near the Wind River in Washington; when he caught its eye, it turned and plodded away. In 1960 the president of a Portland heavy-equipment company, fishing in northern California, saw something like a looming ghost in the half light of the forest; apparently it had seen him first, for it was already silently striding away. It left large deep tracks.

In 1967 a logging contractor said he saw three hideous ogrelike things near Round Mountain in Oregon. He swore that they lifted rocks that could have weighed as much as two hundred pounds, from beneath which they dug up and devoured nests of rodents. Years later Byrne sought out the place. He saw thirty odd-looking holes in the high broken ridges thereabouts, among rocks that did weigh two to three hundred pounds. The rodents of that area were marmots, or woodchucks. In October, when the logger allegedly saw the three giants, marmots are already in deep hibernation and can be handled without their awakening.

In 1969 four young people, driving to Portland, saw what they took to be Bigfoot mount a high rocky bluff near The Dalles at 5:00 A.M. They stopped and peered up at it for several minutes, but it was still squatting there when they left. In 1970—again by dawn light— a fire lookout in a tower near Oregon's lonely Timothy Lake saw an awful creature stroll up the road toward the tower, but it suddenly turned off and was not seen again. In 1971 a deputy sheriff saw a shaggy man-thing shambling along a forest road in Grays Harbor County, Washington. He sat entranced until it lumbered away through the trees.

The most exciting and convincing encounter, I

thought, took place in 1974 in the blue-green silence of the Hood River forest, about thirty miles west of The Dalles. We found two participants who told their story for my television series.

One May morning Jack Cochran, a forty-three-year-old logger from nearby Parksdale, was in the cab of his logging crane. Out of the corner of his eye he noticed movement at the edge of the trees, which was unusual, because no one was supposed to be there.

A crane operator has to watch for people. If he makes a false move with one of the ponderous loads that a crane swings through the air, he can crush someone. So Cochran looked again.

"I saw these two long legs moving at the edge of the timber," he told our interviewer. "Our catskinner is a young fellow, he has fairly long legs, and I asked myself, 'What's Tom doing over there in the woods?' But then I saw Tom behind me in the clearing where he should be. So who was it? I swung the boom around to see better."

As soon as he saw the visitor more clearly, Cochran cut his engine and jumped from the cab. He has sharp eyes; when he isn't working in the woods he is hunting, or sketching wild animals, or woodcarving. The figure he saw was massively built, particularly in the shoulders. It was covered with thick black hair, and stood about six and a half feet tall. Arms hanging at its sides, it stood watching him.

"A chill went up my back," he recalled. "I thought, 'By God, it must be Bigfoot!' Then it turned and walked away—gracefully, like an athlete, with long gliding strides. It reached an arm out and kind of tested the trees as it walked by. It just moved off down the hill."

Cochran was asked to describe the creature.

"I never actually saw his face. But his head seemed to just spring up out of his shoulders, no neck. The arms were long in proportion to a human's. They hung out like a human's, not forward like a bear's."

His two companions didn't see the passerby. The next day, however, during a work break the pair stepped into the shade of the forest edge. Suddenly a huge shape rose out of the bushes and quickly walked away from them.

Fermin Osborne wanted to get a better look at it. He ran after it, leaving young Tom standing agape.

Osborne, a logger from Tennessee, told us, "Oh, he was a big, broad-shouldered, hairy-looking thing. I was surprised how fast he was getting away. When he turned over the ridge there, I lost him. I rolled a couple of big boulders down the hill, thought maybe I'd scare him out and get another better look. But we never saw him again. He had a short, short neck and real broad shoulders, real dark hair all over. Some kind of a god-damn monster. All the time I've been in the woods I never met anything like that."

Byrne heard of these incidents the next day, and hurried there with a team of volunteer investigators. They found deep scuff marks and indentations in the soil, and the boot prints where Osborne had run after the creature, and the two hollows where he had picked up the rocks that he rolled. Here and there were broken twigs, perhaps crushed under the weight of a soft but heavy foot, and stones loosened by a similar weight. The ground wasn't firm enough to register clear tracks, but there was no doubt that something awesome had passed that way.

After I had read reports awhile, it struck me that from 1886 on they had one aspect in common: Whether observed or tracked, the monsters of these mountains did nothing very dramatic. They didn't charge, jump, stomp, roar, glare, throw things, or menace anyone. They simply stood staring, or turned and went away sedately, almost decorously.

Few hallucinations could be that tame. Hoaxes likewise.

Fabricated stories tend to be richly circumstantial. If a yarn is about a forest monster, surely the fantasized thing would sound more credible on all fours part of the time, as apes and monkeys are; yet this persuasive detail is never added. Bigfoot or Sasquatch always squats, stands, and walks (never running at all) on two large flat feet. Thus, potentially good stories are spoiled by dullness. I couldn't help thinking that the tellers of all these tales were singularly lacking in creative wit—unless, of course, their tales were true.

Another question nagged at me. There was only one piece of film (except for a few obvious trick shots) that seemed to show Bigfoot—the twenty-eight-foot strip taken by Patterson in 1967. Its authenticity had been under suspicion ever since. If there was any real chance that it could be exposed as a fake, I did not want to risk attack by showing it on my TV series.

Byrne was ninety-five-percent sure that Patterson's pictures were genuine. "The site of the footage was highly visible—and highly vulnerable for a hoaxer," he said. "On any weekend, one was liable to encounter small groups from Hoopa, or from Willow Creek or even further, driving in and hoping to get a look at Bigfoot. A hoax party could easily be surprised by a car on either of two roads. There were good film sites further up the stream, offering heavier cover and closed surroundings that would protect hoaxers against surprise during the elaborate preparations they would have had to make.

"Two more points stand in favor of the footage," he went on. "In separate statements, both men said the shots were taken around one-thirty on a Friday afternoon. Friday is when people like to get off from work early and out for the weekend. They pack their gear and head into the woods. It is the most dangerous time of the week to try a fake. Look, Gimlin and Patterson had spent years searching for a Bigfoot. If the shot was faked, they must have been planning it for a long time. Making the fur suit alone would have taken tedious and painstaking work. On the big day, surely they would choose a better site. The arrival of just one car would have spoiled all their plans. . . . Another point is that Patterson needed money badly a year before he died. If he were a faker, he would have come forth with some new 'discovery' to mend his fortunes."

I respected Byrne's reasoning, but I needed other expert opinion too. The chief technician at the Walt Disney Studios examined the film and said, "If it's a fake then it's a masterpiece. But the only place in the world where it could be faked is here at Disney. This footage wasn't made here."

Next I phoned Dr. Napier in London. As an anthropologist specializing in the anatomy of ape and human feet, he has been studying photos and casts of Snowman and Bigfoot tracks for twenty years.

"If we confine ourselves to hard evidence, then the answer is clear," he told me. "Bigfoot does not exist. There is no scrap of hard evidence that such creatures are roaming the Himalayas or America's coastal ranges. Nevertheless, there is soft evidence: eyewitness accounts, footprints galore, a few supplementary items such as hairs and droppings. I try to discount eyewitness reports. Footprints are another matter.

"No bear, mountain lion, or other innocent denizen of the forests can be held responsible for this gigantic spoor. There are no wild orangutans in North America, never have been. The evidence convinces me that some of the tracks are real. But the mind starts to boggle at the preposterous idea of creatures eight feet tall stomping barefoot through the forests, unknown to science. I can only say there must be *something* in northwest America that needs explaining, and it leaves manlike footprints."

"Could these prints conceivably be made by unknown members of the human family?"

He hesitated. "If just one track is true-bill, then as scientists we have a lot to explain. Among other things, we shall have to rewrite the story of human evolution—shall have to accept that *Homo sapiens* isn't the only living product of the hominid line—shall have to admit that there are still major mysteries to be solved in a world we thought we knew so well."

This wasn't a direct answer, but he was more forthright than most scientists care to be.

Another anthropologist straddled in similar fashion. Don Abbott of the Provincial Museum in Victoria said of the many Bigfoot tracks, "If the evidence of which I am aware has been the work of hoaxers, it would be one of the most elaborate hoaxes ever perpetrated. I find this possibility almost as incredible as the possibility that such a creature exists."

But at last I met an anthropologist who would say plainly that he believed in mountain monsters: Dr. Grover Krantz in Pullman, Washington.

"I'm satisfied that Patterson's film is a real film of a Sasquatch walking by," he said immediately. "I've examined the film many times, stopped its frames and taken measurements. All the anatomy of the creature is consistent. It just simply doesn't fit with a man wearing a suit.

"The shoulders and chest are too wide. The feet are probably designed for carrying that kind of body weight —which doesn't make sense unless you've got a body of that size. Patterson couldn't have faked this. I talked to him about it and he didn't even understand what I was talking about."

"Then you do accept the idea that Sasquatches are around?"

"Yes. The footprints are the most convincing things. I have a cast here, for instance. It's a cast of a huge, deformed foot—obviously crippled, as shown by these bulges. Probably the foot was crushed in youth. More than five hundred different prints of this crippled foot were found on a half-mile track in 1969. At one point, whatever made the track stepped easily over a fence as high as a man's waist."

I knew what he meant: Why would a hoaxer go to the extra trouble of creating a pathetically malformed foot, and of laying hundreds of prints of it and its normal mate? Why lay them in mountain country where they might not be discovered before the next storm obliterated them?

Dr. Krantz measured the cast for me. It was seventeen and a half inches long, seven inches wide—one of the largest ever found.

He pointed to its two smallest toes, pushed far over to the side of the foot. "These indicate gaps between footbones. Anatomically this implies that the ankle weight has shifted somewhat forward of where it would be in a human foot. The leverage has been redesigned.

And it happens to be redesigned just exactly the way it would have to be for an eight-hundred-pound biped. It's not just a human foot enlarged. So if somebody dreamed up Cripple Foot, it was an anatomist who was a genius, able to create from nothing all the details of how a crushed foot might change to support a body weight several times that of a man. The depth of Cripple Foot's tracks would have required a prankster to carry many hundreds of pounds of extra weight."

I asked him how his scientific colleagues had reacted when he first told about these findings.

"When I decided to talk openly about the Sasquatch, I figured that it would cost me pretty badly in terms of scientific reputation, promotions, raises, things like that. It did cost me, for quite a while. But I thought if I could use my influence to bring out the definitive proof someday, then it would all be worth it.

"As it turns out, I've now gotten a number of scientists to pay attention. So I don't think I'm really losing any more."

I looked around—at his shelves with plaster casts of feet, at photos of tracks, at maps showing where dozens of different reports of the phantom giants had originated. I asked, "What will it take for most of your colleagues to accept the fact that there is indeed a Bigfoot, a Sasquatch?"

"A piece of the body. Nothing else will be accepted. Not even good movies. I would say to anyone gathering Sasquatch information, don't even bother to bring a camera. There is no photograph of the Sasquatch that will convince the skeptical scientists. But if we find bones, the whole thing is settled right there. If we don't, then we'll probably have to kill one, grisly as that sounds."

Later I got to wondering about bones. Why had none ever been found?

Byrne explained to me: "When a wild thing dies, two conditions must be fulfilled if any evidence is to survive. First, the thing must be entombed in a substance that will preserve its remains—sand, lava, tar, peat, ice, for example. Second, preservation must be followed by discovery. Usually this is possible only if erosion, or other natural forces, gives us a great deal of assistance. In the country where Bigfoot lives, these two conditions aren't likely to occur.

"Rain-drenched forests, with winter snows and summer suns, couldn't be much worse for preserving fossils. The soil is warm, moist, and acidic. It just dissolves bones.

He added, "Nature has its own disposal system. Bodies are eaten by other creatures, from bears all the way down to worms and ants. A bear would very likely chew up bones. Ask outdoorsmen if they ever saw a skeleton of a deer or bear or cougar. Few have. So the odds are heavily against finding any part of a dead Bigfoot."

Up there in the wilderness, America's perennial game of hunt-the-monster seems likely to go on forever.

10

Monsters Astray?

Almost no one goes far into Honey Island Swamp, I was told. The story goes that monsters guard the swamp. Monsters who like living flesh in large chunks. Not alligator-type monsters, but something big and bristly and two-legged.

So I knew I had to go there, with a camera crew.

The name, Honey Island Swamp, makes it sound small and perhaps cute. I figured on a few miles of sedge grass and sand scrub and canebrakes, with a hummock in the middle. I was wrong. People there-abouts told me that a man could work his way straight through that swamp for a day and a night without coming out the other side.

To arrive at Honey Island Swamp, we followed the West Pearl River up from New Orleans, winding through oceans of tall saw grass rippling in warm breezes. The swamp lies partly in Mississippi's Pearl River County, partly in the little parishes (counties) alongside the river in Louisiana.

The region is speckled with bayous and swamps, but the Honey Island mire seems to be the only one rumored to contain monster-men. Maybe *rumored* is the wrong word. Even at the edges of the swamp there is no loose talk about monsters. In the nearest towns—Mississippi's Picayune, with a population of seven thousand, and Louisiana's Bogalusa, three times as big—a stranger isn't likely to hear mention of anything huge and unexplained. Modern Americans don't like to be thought superstitious or gullible, even in Cajun country where ghost lore is still believed and voodoo still practiced. But I did gather indirectly that some residents have ventured a little way into Honey Island Swamp, and refuse to do so again.

One of these is Mrs. Perry Lee Ford of Picayune. Even though her husband is six feet six and weighs 320 pounds, she won't go near the swamp with him anymore. Not since what happened there four years ago.

My crew finally got her husband to talk about it. He is twenty-seven, an inspector for an engineering company, a lifelong hunter and fisherman.

"My wife and I were out on a fishing trip," he began, "and we walked across part of the swamp because our boat was missing. High water had gotten it or something. So we had to camp out on the riverbank. About nine o'clock at night I heard this peculiar scream about a half a mile away."

We asked him to describe the scream.

"Well, I guess it kind of starts off like a coyote but it never does come back down. The pitch just stays real high. Extremely loud. Then towards the end of the howl it changes to a snarl, like.

"I never heard nothing like it. It was terrible. It really, really scared my wife. She wanted me to build a big fire. So I went out gathering wood, and it screamed again. This time it was closer, maybe three hundred yards from us. I tried not to let her know it scared me too, so I went ahead and kept on building the fire. Less than ten minutes later it squalled again, right on top of us."

Did they see anything?

"Never did see a thing. It was pitch-black dark.

"Anyway, I built eight fires and we got in the middle of them because it really frightened me. The squalling almost shook the leaves off the trees it was so loud. I had a little four-ten shotgun, but only three shells for it. I shot out through the woods to try to run the thing off. We kept hearing something every now and then, like it was walking, out around us. We had one of them old flashlights but the light wouldn't shine more than fifteen foot out in the woods.

"I've been in the woods all my life, you know, and I never heard anything like that howl and snarl. . . . I spent all last year hunting it, and I might spend quite a few more years, because I sure would like to find it. I tell you the truth, whatever it is I don't believe nobody's ever seen it."

Perry Lee Ford's story was strikingly similar, in a way, to the Bigfoot stories in the Pacific Northwest—simple, without any scary visual details that he might so easily have added if he were trying to make an impression.

But he was mistaken in his belief that nobody has seen the swamp's mysterious inhabitant. A man who lives on the edge of the fen, and goes in often to trap and fish, seventy-two-year-old Ted Williams, will admit when pressed that he has seen a monstrous figure there eight or nine times in the last five years.

"The reason I never did say nothing about it, people don't believe there's anything like that," he told our crew. "I don't like to be called a liar. Nobody do."

Warming to our sympathetic attention, he described what he had seen: About eight hundred pounds of bristle; hands as big as barley forks; a small head and no neck; long hair hanging down over the ears; body broad across the shoulders; about seven feet tall; dark gray wiry hair all over.

"The first time I saw it, it was standing plumb still like a stump, up at my trapline. I stopped and realized it wasn't a stump. When I stopped, it run and jumped a bayou without so much as a grunt. . . . Other times there was two of them. I done everything I could to make them look at me, but they wouldn't. Just run off and I heard them holler. They make different sounds—kind of choking sounds, sometimes I'd say like a cougar. They got an awful scent, worse than a skunk to my thinking. You can smell the stink for a quarter of a mile."

I mentioned the unspoken fear of the swamp that

I'd sensed among people who lived near it. Ted Williams had no such fear.

"They're not dangerous," he said of the nameless giants he had seen. "They don't want to bother nobody. They never have bothered me when I was out walking. They run.

"One time me and another fellow heard a terrible noise inside a thicket. I said, 'They things are killing some hogs in there now. Hear 'em squealing, hear 'em a-beating the hogs just like with a stick.' After a while it quieted down. I reckon they eat 'em, don't know what else they'd do. I heard 'em wading in the water but never did see them, it was too thick in the place where we were. The feller that was with me said, 'That's a horse, you hear him neighing?' I said, 'There's two of 'em if you'll listen. They keeping in contact. That water is fifteen feet deep where they is now.'"

The old trapper went on to recount that he and his companion finally went into the thicket. "We found where they killed three big hogs and ate 'em. That was the most blood I ever saw in my life, all over the timber and brush and briers, and the water about this deep full of blood."

Another man who claims to have seen something peculiar in Honey Island Swamp is Arnold Gibson. He has lived in southern Mississippi all his life, and spends his days in the woods estimating timber for loggers. About a year ago, according to Gibson, he was driving his pickup truck on a logging road that zigzags through a corner of the swamp.

"I just glanced out of the pickup and seen something to the side of the road," he recalled. "I don't know, it didn't look like no man. Just a big old hairy thing, better'n six feet. It was standing. But it wouldn't have been a bear. I got up 'side him, and he turned and wheeled, went off fast through the woods, and I didn't get a good look at his face. I think I scared him as much as he did me. I come on out.

"I tell you, I don't know about that thing. It just put a funny feeling on me. When I drive that road now, I'm always looking for him, real careful."

These three interviews convinced me that Honey Island Swamp might be more than a setting for tall tales or optical illusions. The straightforward stories of Ford and Williams and Gibson tended to confirm one another.

They all implied a bestial thing akin to the Snowman and Bigfoot. Maybe the same kind of monstrous hominid or humanoid had spread through parts of the New World a million years or more before the more versatile *Homo sapiens* migrated east and south from Siberia and drove most large living things into hiding or extinction.

I wanted to probe further into whatever the swamp held. I asked my associates to arrange an expedition, preferably with someone who not only knew the marshland well but had seen an unidentified ogre there. Such arrangements would obviously take time. Most people's courage and talkativeness seemed to ebb when we broached the subject of a trip into the swamp.

While waiting for the right contacts to be made, I delved deeper into what science knew of giant man-things.

Loren Eiseley, one of the most prominent anthropologists, wrote recently, "Through the past few decades the labors of pioneer scientists have succeeded in turning up amid ancient cave deposits a hitherto unsuspected group of ape-men or man-apes. . . . The number of forms and datings could only suggest that not all of them were direct human ancestors. These creatures hinted rather of a variety of early man-apes, not all of whom had necessarily taken the final step of becoming human. . . . The simplified versions of single-line human evolution were very unlikely to be true."

Presumably, one of the scientists Eiseley had in mind was Ralph von Koenigswald, a Dutch paleontologist who opened new dimensions in the story of evolution when he made a discovery in a Chinese drugstore. He eventually led most anthropologists to a supposition that would have seemed unthinkable to Darwin: there may have been at least two separate human species. (And may still be, some monster enthusiasts maintain.)

He was in Hong Kong in 1934. Passing a drugstore, he stepped in to pick over whatever bones it might purvey. Fossil hunters in the Far East made a point of browsing in apothecary shops. Chinese doctors esteemed the curative powers of "dragon bones," which are fossil bones and teeth of many kinds, pounded into powder and taken internally. Therefore, Chinese pharmacists throughout the Orient paid well for fossils. As a student, von Koenigswald had examined a large collection of fossil teeth in the Munich Museum, amassed in the 1900s from pharmacies all over China.

On this particular day, he noticed a jar of teeth on the drugstore counter. While waiting to be served, he spread out a handful, and amused himself trying to determine what animals the teeth had belonged to.

Suddenly he stared, then carefully picked up one tooth. He knew it was a third lower molar, but he had never before seen any tooth of that size. It was nearly an inch from front to back—six times larger than a human molar. Although it was worn down and the roots were missing, he was able to identify it as belonging to some kind of primate. (Primates are the order to which man and apes belong.)

But what primate? Its owner, if proportionately as big as the tooth, must have been much larger than the largest known gorilla. The biggest ape teeth ever found were only half the size of the piece of yellowed ivory he held in his fingers.

He asked the druggist where the tooth had come from. The man had no idea. It had been in the shop a very long time. His father or grandfather might have bought it originally. Or it could have been collected even further back in his family's history, when his ancestors often found dragon teeth while digging in the fields.

Frustrated, von Koenigswald canvassed every drugstore in Hong Kong. No more giant molars.

He went upriver to Canton. There he eventually came across another tooth like the one in Hong Kong; this time it was an upper molar. He kept searching, and in 1939 found a third molar, in a better state of preservation than the other two. Its crown and root were intact.

All three specimens were about the same size—so von Koenigswald realized that he must be collecting teeth of the largest primate that ever lived. He named the newly discovered creature *Gigantopithecus*, or "giant ape."

When Japan invaded the Dutch East Indies during World War II, von Koenigswald was interned as an enemy alien. At about the same time, the brilliant and controversial Franz Weidenreich, a student of fossil man, decided that the teeth were not those of a giant ape, but of a giant man, "and should therefore have been named *Gigantanthropus* (giant man)."

He thought the teeth could be related to a puzzling fragment of jawbone that von Koenigswald had found in Java. The jawbone also seemed to indicate that its owner had been a man of gigantic stature—between eight and twelve feet tall. This led to the sensational inference that modern man had evolved from earlier giant forms by a process of shrinkage through millions of years.

"I believe that all these [giant] forms have to be ranged back in the human line," he wrote, "and that the human line leads to giants, the farther back it is traced. . . . In other words, the giants may be directly ancestral to man."

When von Koenigswald was set free after the war, he disagreed with Weidenreich's theory, and began combing the Orient for more *Gigantopithecus* teeth. By 1954 he had nineteen. Meanwhile, China's top pale-ontologist, Pei Wen-Chung, arranged with the national government to screen all pharmaceutical assortments of "dragon bones" for unusual fossil specimens. This brought forty-seven of the mysterious giant teeth from two of China's southern provinces in 1955. The search for the origin of the giants was narrowing.

On close study the teeth proved to be virtual dupli-cates of human teeth enlarged sixfold. So von Koenigs-wald reversed his earlier stand, and decided that the giants might belong to what he loosely termed "the human group." They probably lived half a million to a million years ago, he said. However, an almost identical jawbone, at least five million years old, turned up in India. So *Gigantopithecus* must have flourished for a long, long time.

Chinese paleontologists were agog. They sent expeditions to dig in limestone cliffs of Kwangsi Chuang, hoping to find full skeletons of the giants. By 1958 they had unearthed another enormous jaw.

A farmer named Chin Hsiu-huai, collecting fertilizer in a mountain cave nearby, found still another large jaw, with some teeth still attached. He had heard of the Peking scientists' quest, so he took the jaw to them. His sons even searched the fields where they had scattered the fertilizer, and retrieved more teeth that had fallen out of the jawbone.

These finds apparently pinpointed an area where *Gigantopithecus* had lived. Excavating furiously, the scientists added two more jaws and about a thousand isolated teeth to their inventory of *Gigantopithecus* fossils. By this time they felt they had a plethora of teeth and jaws, and were baffled by their failure to find any other skeletal parts of the massive creatures. Why did this rich fossil site yield no skulls, no bits of bone from arms or legs or torsos?

Investigators eventually hit on several theories. The Kwangsi Chuang deposits looked like the kind of bone piles that are accumulated by predators. Even now, in parts of Asia, wild dogs live in caves and hunt by packs, as they probably did millions of years ago. They sometimes bring down bears, tigers, and leopards. Perhaps the giant bipeds were their prey too.

Another possibility was that the Kwangsi Chuang bone piles were the leftover contents of porcupine burrows; many of the fossils showed abrasions that hinted that porcupines had gnawed the bones for their calcium content, and a number of the teeth had had their roots carefully chewed away. If primeval porcupines relished jaws, they probably dragged these to their burrow and left all other bones wherever the giants fell.

At any rate, intensive study of the teeth and jaws gradually convinced anthropologists that the creatures were quite different from gorillas, the largest primates known to science. Certain dental peculiarities indicated that the giants probably bolted enormous quantities of raw meat. "Feeding habits involved little preparatory nipping or shredding," one expert wrote. "Shredding in particular plays an important role in the feeding of living apes."

Whether ape or man, there had definitely been a huge (and presumably hairy) two-legged predator in Asia, at least roughly in the same area from which Abominable Snowman sightings were reported. If *Gigantopithecus* or some altered form of it survived unseen in mountains and forests until the present day, it could account for the Snowman stories.

The primordial man-ape's main occupation must have been hunting. If his overall proportions were in keeping with his jaw, the creature should have weighed about six hundred pounds and stood nine feet tall. He would have had to be a heavy eater to nourish himself adequately. Just behind any rock he might encounter such enemies as the saber-toothed tiger and the great cave bear, which reared to a height of sixteen feet on its hind legs.

There may have been titanic fights between these monsters. If *Gigantopithecus* ever learned to use a club, he could have swung one heavy enough to crush a tiger's skull as it sprang, or beat off a bear and brain him. His enormous teeth were efficient tools not only for ripping out chunks of his prey but also for gnawing off a big tree limb for a cudgel. On the other hand, if he lacked the intelligence required to club or stone his enemies, he probably had to seek refuge in mountains or at least deserted hideaways. We know that his species had four million years for dispersal and mutation.

There is tantalizing evidence for the survival of outsize apes in China. As far as we know, the last *Gigantopithecus* died at least a half million years ago. But around 400 B.C. the philosopher Hsün Tzu recorded that man-sized hairy apes lived in the Yellow River Valley—and stood erect instead of going on all fours as other apes did.

Apes were known in northern Sinkiang Uighur near Tibet as recently as two thousand years ago. A Tibetan book contains a picture of what looks like an upright ape. The caption says, "This wild man lives in the mountains. His body resembles that of a man, and he has enormous strength." Sinkiang Uighur and Tibet are very close to legendary Abominable Snowman country. They also are near the area where the giant panda was able to hide from science until this century—and where it was hunted for more than seventy years on the strength of rumor before the first specimen was captured.

If the panda could hide, why not the Snowman?

Why not Bigfoot and the monsters of Honey Island Swamp?

Why shouldn't all these be variants of the supposedly extinct *Gigantopithecus*?

As Loren Eiseley pointed out, human evolution can't now be considered a simple straight line of descent. Several different human or near-human types lived simultaneously, at least in China and probably elsewhere. Africa has yielded the fossils of a bewildering assortment of manlike bipeds who seem to have existed as neighbors for thousands of years.

In Europe the famous Neanderthal man knew and competed with our own "modern" species. Anthropologists used to think that Neanderthal man was a sort of apish evolutionary dead end that had lived only in Europe during the Ice Age. We now know that Neanderthal types were widespread. Moreover, they were closely related to modern man, and were not just a long-ago offshoot from the same line.

Neanderthal man seems to have flourished until the end of the Ice Age, then died out. Why? The usual assumption is that somehow he wasn't "fit" to survive. But this conflicts with known facts, because Neanderthal man had an even larger brain than ours, and his tools and weapons were at least equal to those of early "modern" man. Besides, Neanderthal man had already survived the terrible privation of several glacial advances and retreats. How would this hardy chap suddenly become unfit?

According to another theory, our ancestors sprang up somewhere in the Middle East (where the biblical Garden of Eden has been placed by some archaeologists) and then spread into areas occupied by the Neanderthals. As we are painfully aware, we are an aggressive breed. Our ancestors, presumably just as bloodthirsty, could have exterminated the less predatory Neanderthals and all other near-human types such as *Gigantopithecus*.

I've often wondered if a primeval competition between two closely related types of human beings was retold symbolically in the struggle between Esau and Jacob described in Genesis. Esau was said (25:25) to be "all over like a hairy garment," and later Jacob remarked (27:11), "Behold, Esau my brother is a hairy man, and I am a smooth man." Esau seemed to live outdoors, "a hunter," while Jacob dwelt in tents. Esau's robe had a singular and powerful odor, which brings to mind the strong smell so often mentioned in connection with the alleged monsters in our mountains and swamps.

The Bible mentions other wild hairy beings. When Saint Jerome translated the Bible from Hebrew to Latin, he translated a Hebrew word meaning "demon" to a Latin word meaning "hairy one." The prophet Isaiah foretold Babylon in ruins, and Jerome translated part of this prophecy as "The hairy ones shall dance there." In another of Isaiah's predictions of destruction, Jerome wrote, "One hairy creature will shout to the other." We can't be sure what Isaiah meant, but some scholars think that the Hebrew demon was, as Jerome implied, a hairy two-legged horror that lurked in deserted and ruined places.

The most famous Sumerian myth tells of a hairy wild man who lived among beasts. He was called Enkidu. He defeated Gilgamesh (the hero of the myth) in wrestling, then became his fast friend, but the gods

condemned Enkidu to death for slaying a sacred bull.
Grief over Enkidu's death led Gilgamesh into his epic
search for the secret of eternal life.

We also find hairy lawless man-things in classical
myths. Tales of a Greek god Silenus describe him as
fierce, strong, and wild. He uprooted a tree for a
weapon. Painters and sculptors portrayed him as hair-
covered. When an actor played Silenus in dramas his
costume was a shaggy garment.

Silenus didn't really originate with the Greeks. He
seems to have been a personification of the sileni, a
tribe of wild forest spirits who were part of the mythology of the Phrygians of Asia Minor.

The Romans had a shaggy wild god too. He was
Silvanus, a dangerous and unpredictable deity who
lived in forests and mountains. He ruled all lands outside the fringe of cultivation. An ancient statue shows
him carrying a tree in his left hand. In early Roman
days he was sometimes called Silvanus, sometimes
Mars—whose character we know well, and who later
developed into a separate god.

Medieval European legends told of wild, hairy, manlike beings in the Orient, particularly in India. Roger
Bacon, one of the best-educated scholars in thirteenth-
century Europe, was sure that hairy wild men were no
myth. He wrote that in the "high rocks" of Tibet and
China there dwelt a hairy apelike creature. Perhaps this
was the first English reference to the Snowman story.

Today the Soviets seem to think the Snowman is
some strange sort of prehistoric man, which they call
an alma. An officer in the czarist army reported seeing
an alma in 1870. Mongol tribesmen have talked of
almas for generations. The Soviets got interested
enough to send an expedition into the Caucasus Mountains in search of almas in 1958, with results that they
characteristically kept secret. However, a 1964 publication quoted a Professor Porschnev as saying that two
hominid skulls were found in Mongolia: "The skulls
were exactly where scores of people, from shepherds
and milkmaids to local authorities, had reported seeing
these terrifying and remarkable bipeds."

Professor Dmitri Bayanov, an authority on hominids, predicted that another expedition, organized in 1974, would probably continue its surveys for several years. The expedition was led by Professor Jeanne Koffman, a Frenchwoman who became a Soviet citizen during the Second World War and is a member of the Soviet Geographical Society. She and her crew planned to camp in the Caucasus Mountains through winter months, on the chance of making contact with almas. The Soviets are said to think that their almas, the yeti or Snowman, and the Bigfoot or Sasquatch may all be remnants of a race of dawn men who somehow managed to survive into this century.

And so out of the ancient darkness of superstition and myth the hairy man-monsters have come to our times. Recent reports of them haven't been confined to the United States and Canada. In the forests of Indonesia there is rumored to be a manlike monster called an *orang pendek*. Jesuit missionaries to South America have brought back stories of shadowy giants seen striding through certain jungle areas.

The southern Florida swamplands are said to harbor big-footed things known locally as "skunk-apes," but their tracks indicate two species: the larger one has three toes and a violent nature, while the smaller five-toed kind is shy and harmless. Plaster casts of both types of tracks have been taken, and more than a hundred sightings of skunk-apes have been reported in the Everglades during the past five years. But the Everglades are just too huge for us to send in camera crews on the chance of a lucky shot.

The Honey Island Swamp is fairly large, but our chances seemed better. We finally found someone who would lead us into the heart of it, and who had personally encountered monsters there. His name is Harlan Ford. He had been a traffic controller for the Federal Aviation Agency but had quit at a comparatively young age. Now fifty, he has lived near the swamp for more than twenty years, supporting his wife and three children by hunting and fishing and part-time contracting jobs.

In 1962 he and a crony, Billy Mills, built themselves a little cabin in "a real remote area back in that swamp." One sunny morning they were taking supplies in when they both got a feeling that something formidable was nearby.

Mills thought he saw the bushes move, and Ford told him to keep a sharp look-out. It couldn't be a man, they were sure, but they were sure that something was there. Mills thought it might be a big hog or a bear.

They moved ahead cautiously, keeping their eyes on the creature. It was on all fours and seemed to be rooting in the mud. When they were about thirty feet away, it turned and saw them, then rose onto two feet as a human would. It had dingy grayish bristle all over, but its squarish face seemed almost human. Its chest and shoulders were huge.

Ford and Mills stood frozen. The creature stared for a moment, then plunged into the bushes and disappeared.

"We didn't tell anybody, because we knew we'd seen something out of the ordinary," Ford explained to me. "We were bound and determined to kill it. We went back with buckshot for I'd say two or three months, and laid in there, but for the rest of that season we didn't see it anymore."

I hoped he would see it this time, with my camera crew along.

The brown river led through the fens like an aisle. When we had poled a short way, it was as though a door closed behind us, shutting out the world. Timelessness hung like a vacuum over that trackless unvisited wilderness. Honey Island Swamp looked just as it must have looked from the beginning.

It was awesome with great gloomy trees. Rattan vines linked the trees in webs that might have been spun by spiders from the age of mastodons. Cane grew rooftop-tall in brakes as dense as fur, right down to the water's edge.

As we penetrated farther the trees grew taller, giving me a feeling of descending an ever-deepening and darkening canyon. Each twist in the river carried us

farther from all that I knew and was. Even the occasional cries of birds and animals were strange; surely
they came from creatures unlike those in aviaries and
zoos. But Ford said the tracks I saw occasionally were
those of deer, bear, muskrat, wild turkey, and hordes
of rats, mice, frogs, and turtles.

At last we stopped. We set up camera and mike,
and Ford began talking.

"At this time we're standing well within the interior
of Honey Island Swamp, and you can tell by its surroundings here it's a pretty desolate area," he said,
looking straight into the camera. "I'd say there's spots
in here that no white man ever walked on. Whatever
it is that exists in here—I don't say it's a monster, I
don't know what it is—but whatever this is, if it prowls
and continues to prowl at night in a swamp this huge,
it could stay in here another two or three hundred
years and not be located."

He went on to tell about his first encounter with the
thing. "It was in this area right here. Got right on top
of him. . . . And later, going to the camp, coming
through this little ravine bottom and this wet ground,
is where we first found his tracks. We immediately went
on back and got plaster of paris and began pouring in
his tracks. We saw quite a number of tracks right along
this edge, but at no time did we find any tracks where
it had gone in the water. I guess it would let down to
drink, and that's where we would find the heavy clawed
front feet, or hands, of this creature."

I asked him if all the tracks were made by one particular big-footed being.

"An archaeologist that has poured some of these
tracks with me claims to have five different sets. One
track had a broken toe, and a knuckle receded back
into its paw or whatever you would call it. Fresh tracks
four times in forty-two days, right in this area. And
that about wraps this particular spot up."

We pushed deeper into a maze of muddy water,
hummocks, and little jungles of cypress and oak and
elm. Strangler figs choked the trees they climbed on.
Thickets of something-or-other flaunted amazingly

twisted branches and wide leaves with blood-red veins. The monstrous gumbo limbo sent out horizontal branches that billowed like huge fire hoses.

We stopped and set up again. I gave Ford a leading question. "Have you had any sightings during hunting trips?"

"Well, we got too close on it about three years ago during duck season. Really too close, I think. We had approached one of these swamp lakes, and we saw ripples on the water underneath a big oak tree, and that was a sure sign of wood ducks diving. So we got down and crawled out toward that bank. But when we got there it wasn't duck. It was a big wild boar.

"Oh, he had some big tusks on him," he continued. "But he was ripped up and dying. His throat had been torn out. His back leg was still kicking, causing the ripples in the water, and there was blood still dripping off the bushes all around. Whatever killed it, we think we ran it off. Of course we pulled out, right then. We figured we was too close on him."

I asked about night-time experiences.

"One night in there at our camp site, the doggone thing came real close to the camp and its eyes shined. A friend of mine shot at it twice, claimed to hit it, but didn't so much as knock off a bristle. I know because we didn't find any blood the next day. There were guys in there hunting wild hogs with dogs, and we put 'em onto the tracks—and the dogs refused to trail. Just wouldn't."

"Does this thing make any noise?"

"It's got one of the most hideous calls you ever heard in your life. Starts off with a high long scream, and ends with a gurgling-type noise. Very scary. We don't sleep in that camp without a nylon rope on the door, and a loaded gun."

On the way out, we climbed to a hilltop and set up for one final sequence for the TV show.

"The bluff over here borders this West Pearl River," Ford said. "From this vantage point you're able to see a lot of the area where this thing has been sighted. If you look downriver you see a bluff where a friend of mine with the federal government, Jim Harzog, shot at this thing twice." He pointed.

"He says he saw it plain as day, came face to face with it. He described it as something like an ape, about seven foot tall, bristles like tenpenny nails all down its body. He fired on it. It turned and ran and he shot again, but we went back and checked for blood—didn't find any. So we figure Jim missed. It give us the slip again."

He turned and pointed in another direction.

"Now, around this bend that we're looking at is a huge sandbar. The last sign that anybody had of this creature was on this sandbar, where the thing crossed and left footprints found by a member of the Louisiana Wildlife Commission. And that is the very last account we've had, about four months ago."

And so we came out to the twentieth century again. Other men from time immemorial had cautiously avoided this swamp. With better luck we might have seen and photographed whatever horrendous mistake of nature they had feared to meet. But it was not to be. I have still to get my first good look at a legendary monster.

Nevertheless, I think there are monsters in that swamp—and maybe in other swamps. Most of America's swamps have been drained now, for factories and shopping malls and suburbs. But some, like Honey Island, have survived because they are far from population centers. Any swamp could have been a good refuge for any Bigfoot or Snowman who strayed south from the mountains a million years ago. The vastness of forest areas, too, would have offered countless hiding places. Until modern times our continent had a thin *Homo sapiens* population. After the end of the Ice Age there were few large predators on the continent to disturb this shy giant.

Therefore, it may be that *Gigantopithecus,* or something like him, still lives—free as the beasts, and an affront to science—in various secluded pockets of wilderness across North and South America.

I hope he is never caught and dragged into zoos.

There he would be just another Latin name to list in our scientific catalogs. We would gain in knowledge but lose something in spirit.

As long as the giant is at large and uncataloged, revealing himself but briefly, he remains a powerful and shimmering symbol of gaps in our knowledge—a mystifying remainder that the human family tree may still have branches we haven't seen. Undetected, he is good for us. He will not let us feel too complacent.

11

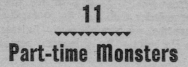

Part-time Monsters

A changed look on Prince Vlad's face, a sudden widening of the eyes, warned me. "You find the smell unpleasant?" he asked very gently, very softly.

I jerked the handkerchief away from my nose and mumbled something. Vlad could scarcely have accepted it as a denial, for I was trying to suppress nausea, which must have shown.

Putting down his fork, the prince stroked his thin mustache thoughtfully. All the while he kept me fixed with a dark twinkling gaze. His eyes were like black beads floating in yellow oil.

At last he said, "I cannot allow your sensitive nose to be offended. I will put you way up high, where the odor does not reach you." He smiled as if he had said something funny. Motioning to a soldier, he drawled, "Take this gentleman away. Set him on a much higher stake than the others."

I awoke trembling, with my heart thumping. What a nightmare. It had been entirely too real. I had relived an experience that had actually happened to someone on April 2, 1459, in the city of Brasov in Walachia, a mountain principality of what is now Romania.

And I knew what had happened next, according to contemporary accounts. Prince Vlad's luckless guest was held with his legs wide apart, facilitating entry of a sharp wooden stake that slid up into him until it held all his weight, somewhat as if he was seated on it. The stake was then hoisted high and set in place—so that

161

the guest could look down on similarly impaled victims, but perhaps not smell them.

I sat up, unable to sleep. I was in an enormous brass feather bed in Bucharest's old Athenee Palace Hotel. This was the first night of my trip to Romania to track down possible origins of those ghoulish monsters called vampires and werewolves—but already I had learned more than I really wanted to know.

I had seen a disagreeably lifelike oil portrait of Prince Vlad IV, nicknamed Tepes, which means "the impaler." He had a narrow, sallow face. I had read the facts about his terrible reign from 1455 to 1462, during which he maintained order in his realm by putting thousands of people to death in picturesque ways.

Vlad enjoyed the process of eliminating potential enemies, critics, insufficiently flattering courtiers, and others who caught his attention unfavorably. Sometimes he scheduled impalements or other tortures as dinner-table entertainment. A German writer described him walking under conscious victims who "twisted around and twitched like frogs. After that he spoke: 'Oh, what great gracefulness they show!'"

Vlad was known by another name too: Dracula.

Yes, there was an authentic historical Dracula who made the fictional one seem tame. He was Vlad IV of Walachia.

The old Roman word *draco* meant "dragon," and *dracula* meant "dragon's son." Latin words were familiar to Romanians in medieval times and still are, even though the Romanians speak Slavonic languages; Romanians claim to be descendants of the conquering Romans who ruled there for two centuries, calling the province Dacia; hence, they insist on calling their nation Romania rather than Roumania or Rumania, as it used to be spelled in atlases and encyclopedias. (For similar reasons, the many gypsies thereabouts call themselves people of Romany.)

Why was Tepes, or Vlad IV, known as the Dragon's Son? Because his father, Vlad III, joined the Order of the Dragon, a central European league of kings and princes who hated the Turks' rampant Ottoman Empire. Vlad III put the dragon emblem on his coins and battle flags, and was pleased to call himself Dracul, i.e. the Dragon. His son was equally proud of the Dracula sobriquet.

Dracul was trapped by Sultan Murad in 1444, but got free by giving his adolescent son as hostage. Dracula spent more years as a prisoner than as a ruler.

I didn't discover precisely what happened to him in the grim old Visegrad fortress thirty miles up the Danube from Budapest. Perhaps his long stay was comfortable, for historians say that his jailers gave him small animals to torture for amusement. At any rate, I think the prince was to become an exemplar of Auden's lines:

> Those to whom evil is done
> Do evil in return.

Dracula was released in 1474 as part of a peace treaty. He soon avenged himself on his captors, with ferocity unequaled until the rise of Hitler and Stalin.

Whenever Turks ventured near his domain, he surrounded them with cavalry, took them prisoner, and spitted them on pikestaffs at his leisure. He waged aggressive wars to capture more Turks. In the course of one campaign he happened to encounter a Turkish envoy who had arranged the trap that led to his long captivity. The envoy had come to Dracula under a pledge of safe conduct, but this made no difference. Dracula immediately set about torturing him—carefully, so that he should always remain conscious. It was said that the luckless emissary took several days to die.

Wholesale, hideous executions earned the Walachian prince his tag "Tepes." According to the Bishop of Erlau, probably the most scholarly and reliable chronicler of that century, Vlad IV authorized the cold-blooded slaughter of approximately one hundred thousand people, including twenty thousand in Brasov on one day. Many were Turks or other outlanders, but he apparently killed at least a tenth of Walachia's population. Impalement was his hobby. He used it in various forms, depending on age, rank, sex, or special circumstances. He usually arrayed the screaming victims neatly in various geometric patterns—often concentric circles around a town, so that townspeople would be aware of them on all sides.

There was head-down impalement on a meat hook, crosswise impalement through the navel, impalement combined with scalping or skinning, and other variations designed to make victims last longer and writhe more entertainingly. On one occasion a red-hot spear was run adroitly up through the intestines until it emerged from the blubbering mouth.

Even so, Dracula occasionally grew bored with skewering people, and tried other divertissements. He forced a husband to eat his wife's breasts. He boiled people alive, one limb at a time. He slit them down the middle.

Once he was annoyed by beggars, so he rounded up all the mendicants in Walachia, set out a feast for them, then burned them alive at their banquet table. Once a delegation of Turkish diplomats wore fezzes in accordance with their native custom while salaaming to Dracula; as a way of showing that he preferred visitors to be bareheaded, the prince ordered the fezzes nailed to their heads.

Vlad was surely gruesome, but none of the chronicles hinted that he might have been a vampire. I wanted to follow Vlad's track, see the places where he had thrived, and try to ascertain the connection if any between him and the Transylvanian vampire legends.

Romania, like all its neighbors, is rigidly communist. Nevertheless, I managed to secure the necessary passport visas, and journeyed from West Germany through Czechoslovakia and Hungary to Romania. It wasn't a happy trip. Central European cities tend to be drab, heavy, and gloomy. The massive masonry of the medieval piles weighed me down; windows were slits in ancient walls three feet thick, and iron-barred. These were cities of ogres' towers, of dungeons and dormers, casements and embrasures, posterns and wickets and drawbridges.

Long black alleys were full of shadows and smells. The dun walls and flat roofs of the more modern apartment buildings put me in mind of barracks. In railroad stations the shrieks of the old locomotives echoed like witches' howls; almost the only other sounds were the clumping of nailed boots on flagstone as a police patrol came through, and the occasional jingle and clash of accouterments as an army regiment moved out for duty in the hinterlands.

Romania had a history of stern repression by its own Iron Guard before it became the most regimented and conventional of all communist nations. But its capital, Bucharest, struck me as happier and more relaxed, at least on the surface, than Prague or Budapest. It had fewer great gray fortress buildings. It had music and wine and good food. I saw swarthy, colorful gypsies here and there.

Strolling through the city, I felt faint tingles of the romantic and the occult. The broad main thoroughfare, Victory Street, was almost deserted. I left it and wandered down ancient, tired alleys with tiny tired houses built into the masonry of quays and bridges—houses that leaned to one another for support, the ancient leaning on the ancient. In my mind I peopled them with fusty, bearded alchemists at their caldrons and crucibles, or aged crones chanting mystic rhymes.

That evening Bucharest was cloaked in mist. The empty streets glistened, and a few streetlamps looked like globular yellow drops suspended against the dark air shimmering with rain. In the dimness the roofs were almost powdery blue, a few lighted windows under them. Intermittently a cloak of fog altered shapes of towered churches, making them loom larger and more strange and mysterious. Sometimes the spiny pinnacles of the old Domnita Baleasa Church in the central square, opposite the still more ancient Palace of Justice, vanished into gray boiling mists, and then my imagination took over and I envisioned them as ghosts' labyrinths. But I still couldn't people the streets with invisible vampires or werewolves.

This had been Dracula's city. He had fortified it and made it the capital of Walachia. But nothing of him lingered in the atmosphere. To get a feel for him, I would have to go to big dark castles in the Carpathian Mountains and perhaps the Transylvanian Alps, where Bram Stoker imagined the literary Dracula to have been. I started before sunrise for Romania's little-known, little-traveled mountains.

Not only the novel but the stage play and the movies about Count Dracula were laid in Transylvania. The name means "land beyond the forest," and at first I had assumed, like many Americans, that Transylvania was an imaginary kingdom in the same Middle European cloudland as the mythical Graustark and Ruritania. But I learned that Transylvania is real. It was part of Hungary for almost a thousand years, until Romania seized it after the First World War. And it was still rich in folklore of werewolves and vampires.

In the dawn, all the mountain line to the north was black and hard like the end of the known world. I shivered a little. Here I was close to the edge, the place where the water gathers speed and goes over the black cliff.

The sun came up very slowly, and for a moment it turned everything red, like blood, before it came flooding down into the grain fields. All through that long day, as I drove up through one village after another, I found that belief in ghouls grew stronger the deeper I went into the mountains. That a person may die and yet live on as a corpse, may sustain himself by sucking blood from the living, seemed to be a fact of life to the rural folk—a fact attested to by parents and grandparents, by wise men and priests.

Long ago, superstitions about vampires were nearly universal. I knew that folklorists had found legends of blood-sucking human monsters in chronicles of ancient Babylon, in India and China, in large stretches of the primitive world. Vampires were cited among the dead in Egyptian scrolls. Montague Summers, an eccentric but eminent English scholar, unearthed so many vampire stories that he devoted two large volumes to them. He said that the ancient Greeks believed in vampires, and that the barbarians picked up this part of Greek culture and spread it over Europe.

Vampires, in ancient belief, were malign spirits who left their graves at night in a kind of somnambulistic trance, prowling in search of stray people whose throats they might pierce with their teeth in order to drink their blood. The corpse of a vampire was always fresh, and could only be put to rest by impalement or burning.

Medieval European chronicles were full of accounts of villagers exhuming corpses and staking them down to keep them in their graves. Not until 1823 did England outlaw the practice of pounding stakes through the hearts of suicide victims. (Suicide victims were considered especially prone to vampirism, as were criminals, bastards, and excommunicated people.)

Perhaps, I thought, the notion behind vampirism could be traced all the way back to the dawn men—to Stone Age hunters, who noticed that when blood poured out of a wounded beast or a fellow human, life too drained away. Blood could have seemed to them a life-giving fluid. We know that primitive people sometimes smeared themselves with blood and sometimes drank it. Deuteronomy 12:23 asserts, "The blood is the life," and Count Dracula quoted this biblical scrap in Stoker's novel.

According to Eastern Orthodox doctrine, the body of anyone bound by a curse will not be received by the earth, will not decay, cannot fully die and find peace. This teaching of the Church naturally fostered the vampire legend in Orthodox countries such as Romania.

In fact, the legend fits in smoothly with other beliefs that date back to pagan times. Romanian villagers like to think their dead are still among them in the parks and streets; life after death is much like life in this sphere, they say. Most of their village cemeteries look like chaotic harbors with gravestones tipped up every which way like sinking ships. This is because the markers settle into the soft soil. But to villagers it is proof that bodies climb from graves.

However, no one thinks that the walking dead are necessarily vampires thirsting for blood. I heard the word *moroi* ("undead") much more often than the harsher epithets *strigoi, vukodlak,* and *brukolak,* which all mean undead blood-drinkers and troublemakers, i.e. vampires.

In Romania's mountains, where shadows multiply by lamplight and candlelight, where woods and castles are acrawl with specters, the belief in evil must have seemed close to gospel in the fifteenth century. How else explain the triumphant ingrained evil of a sovereign like Prince Vlad IV the Impaler, the Dragon's Son? In such an atmosphere the legends grew, and ultimately endowed Dracula with a strange immortality through Stoker's 1897 novel.

Long before 1897, however, the vampire legend apparently had faded from most of Western Europe. Only in Eastern Christendom did it flourish, sanctioned and encouraged by the priests of the Orthodox Church. There the Christians lived in stark dread of attacks by ghouls.

Most Christians thereabouts still do—as I saw while I worked my way closer to the ruined castle in the mountains where the real Dracula had ruled. I was in fairy-story country, I thought. Not the rainbow country of Walt Disney fairy tales, but the scene of the old German stories with woodcuts. While the sun shines, girls and boys play. But when it starts to go down, and the long shadows begin to creep, all wise children go indoors, and the creatures of the night come out. The little wicked creatures who live in the trunks of trees, and the bats and night birds who talk to one another in whispers, and worst of all the blood-sucking, half-human, vaguely regal night monsters who prey on unguarded sleeping people.

An American traveler told me of an incident on his walking tour through these mountains. He reached a lonely farmhouse and knocked repeatedly on the door, calling out that he would pay for food and shelter. He thought the house must be deserted. But just as he was turning away the door opened cautiously, and a burly peasant poked out a pair of tongs holding a live coal. The American stood speechless. The farmer, pale and goggle-eyed, extended the flaming coal for only a moment, then slammed the door and bolted it.

When the traveler told this story to sophisticated Romanian friends, they explained that there is a belief that when a corpse roams by night, it betakes itself to any house it fancies, and knocks at the door, calling loudly. If the resident answers, he is done for. The vampire will enthrall him, and he himself will become a vampire. But if he does not answer he is safe. And he can drive away the vampire with fire. Hence, the peasants in the mountains never answer if a stranger calls to them after sundown. My American acquaintance had been taken for a vampire.

There were similar beliefs elsewhere. I remembered a tale I had heard on the Greek island of Mykonos. A quarrelsome farmer was murdered in the fields. Two days after his burial, word spread that he was being seen at night, and was playing tricks on people. The priests circulated the report, for it meant that masses would be said. On the tenth day after burial, solemn mass was celebrated, the body was exhumed, and the village butcher cut out its heart. The butcher averred that the body was warm—a sure sign that it was a genuine vampire. But removal of the heart had no effect on the vampire, which continued its prowling as before; everyone had something to tell of its doings. The people were beside themselves with terror, and so many families moved to the neighboring islands that Mykonos was threatened with depopulation. But at last a wise man who knew the ways of vampires advised burning the corpse. A pyre of wood, pitch, and tar was built on a promontory, and there the remnants of the body were cremated. The vampire was seen no more. Mykonos had peace, and ballads were composed in honor of the event.

There are records of a "vampire epidemic" in 1730–32 at the Yugoslav village of Meduegna, near Belgrade.

A young soldier named Arnold Paole, returning from military service in Greece, told the girl to whom he was betrothed that he had been attacked at night by a vampire in Greece, but had located its grave and destroyed it—which should have ended the matter. Nevertheless, he soon died, and then was seen around Meduegna after dark. Ten weeks later, yielding to persistent gossip that people dreamed about him and felt strangely weak the morning after, the church sexton disinterred Paole's body while the villagers watched. The body had fresh blood on its mouth, they all agreed. Army doctors sprinkled it with garlic, which is believed to be a protection against vampires, and drove a stake through its heart.

Notwithstanding this, two years later vampires seemed to become rife in Meduegna. A commission came from Belgrade to investigate. Its report was signed on January 7, 1732, by Drs. Johannes Flickinger, Isaac Seidel, Johann Baumgartner, and military men from the capital. They certified to examining fourteen corpses, all listed and described. Twelve of these corpses, including a girl of ten, were found "unmistakably in the vampire condition." The record doesn't show what was done, but presumably the corpses received the standard treatment for vampires. That ended whatever epidemic was raging.

I drove a lonely road up through the Borgo Pass. Athwart the pass, according to legend, stood Castle Bistrita, where Vlad the Impaler lived for five years. But after his death the Germanic peasants nearby sacked the castle, perhaps in retaliation for Vlad's atrocities against their kinsmen farther south in Brasov and Sibiu. Not a trace remained of the castle. Nor did I sense any hint of the miasma that I sometimes noticed in old places where evil had been strong.

A hundred miles to the southwest I found the forbidding Hunedoara Castle, dating back to 1260. This was the stronghold of the Hunyadi family, where Dracula was received as an honored guest in 1452. It looked much like the description of Castle Dracula in Stoker's novel, with massive walls, battlements, towers, and drawbridge. In its impressive Hall of Knights a portrait of Dracula once hung among its gleaming marble columns. But again I felt no aura, no vibrations.

When I got to the old town of Tirgoviste, which was Walachia's capital for two centuries, I did feel uncomfortable.

Somehow I knew that this had been a city of crafty intrigues and awful cruelties. Guides told me that Dracula's royal court here had been as majestic as Versailles. His palace was set amid gardens so extensive and luxuriant that one Venetian traveler compared Tirgoviste to a "vast gaudy flower house."

I strolled through what little remained of the palace. There wasn't much but the foundation. But as I wandered across one spacious weed-grown floor, groans and screams suddenly swirled up silently around me, seeming to rise from every crack in the old flagstones. I was hearing ghosts again.

Beneath my feet lay the dust of those who had connived and striven and flattered to hold the favor of Vlad Tepes. I felt as though the stones were heaving beneath my feet from the pent-up cries of those who lay beneath. And I caught a flickering mental image of a brutal sadist, smiling as he walked among courtiers here.

This room had been the notorious throne hall, I was told. When Vlad IV ascended its throne in the spring of 1456 he knew himself to be insecure. He was only the latest in a rapid succession of princes; political assassinations were frequent. He evidently decided that he must take deceptive but drastic measures.

He invited several hundred of Walachia's wealthiest boyars (landlords) into the throne hall, then had its exits blocked by soldiers. One by one, most of the noblemen were taken from the room and speedily impaled. Their blackening bodies stood a long time as a warning to others.

It was in this same throne room, too, that Vlad ordered the fezzes of the Turkish plenipotentiaries fastened permanently to their heads, and watched them welter in blood and brains at his feet.

I heard many other stories of incidents in this hall. Some told of intended victims who saved themselves by adroit flattery. Once Vlad received two monks from a distant monastery and proudly showed them rows of impaled bodies in the courtyard and gardens. One monk nodded approvingly and clucked, "You are appointed by God to punish evil-doers." Dracula spared him, but impaled his colleague, who bravely expressed disapproval.

Dracula delighted in interrogating guests, and sparing their lives if he thought they answered well. There was a fairly typical chat in September 1458 when he entertained a Polish aristocrat, Benedict de Boithor. After dinner some servants suddenly brought in a golden spear and planted it directly in front of de Boithor, who watched cautiously. Dracula said, smiling, "Tell me, why do you think I have had this spear set up?"

"My lord, I would guess that some great boyar of the land has attracted your attention," the Pole answered, "and you wish to honor him in some way."

"Fairly spoken. You are the representative of a great country, and I have placed the lance expressly in your honor."

The Pole knew Dracula's reputation for macabre humor, and drew the conclusion that "honor" meant impalement. He talked fast. "My lord, if I have been responsible for something deserving of death, I shall not beg you to spare me, for you are the best judge. You would not be responsible for my death, but I alone."

Dracula laughed. He found the statement both witty and flattering. "Had you not answered me in this fashion, I would truly have impaled you," he said. He pressed gifts on the Pole and sent him home unscathed.

Dracula was a pious man. He built at least four large monasteries, where he became a frequent visitor and patron. He also was amorous, and in the evenings often wandered alone in disguise, seeking the company of beautiful but humble women. Those who became his mistresses usually died wtih their sexual organs torn out.

Wherever I went in the mountains, I asked if the

Dragon's Son was considered a vampire. He had been bloodthirsty enough. Was the famous fictional Dracula modeled after this prince?

Answers always were negative. No evidence indicated that peasants of the fifteenth century, or the twentieth, had any notion that their Dracula was a vampire—or that he became one after he was captured and beheaded by Turkish troops.

The mountain people still know a lot about Dracula. He is a national hero, a brave foe of the Turks, heroic defender of the Christian faith. His cruelties, according to today's official Romanian government propaganda, were more or less justified; usually he impaled criminals and enemies of the state. "The chronicles exaggerate the punishments while forgetting to mention the causes," according to a long memo I received from the government's Ministry of Tourism.

I had an opportunity to travel to the misty foothills of Ceahlau Mountain. There are a great many legends of ghostlike horrors that occur in the fog-laden peaks of the mountain. I interviewed, among others, a Romanian surgeon named Gheorghe Iacomi, who entered the Alphine meadows seeking contact with the myths of peasant shepherds. I learned from Iacomi the legend of a fifteenth-century nobleman named Budu who fell in love with a Romanian princess named Anna. When Budu was killed in battle the grief-stricken Anna pleaded with a powerful witch to bring her lover back from the dead. The witch was successful. She raised Budu from his grave, not as a person but as a ghost. While passing over Mt. Ceahlau, Budu's ghost was struck by the rising sun. He turned into a rock. To this day a megalith at Ceahlau's summit is still known as Budu's Tower. Legends abound, but tales of Dracula as he is described in Western literature are unknown. Peasants have heard little of the British novel that combined their national hero and their national superstition, or of the vastly successful play and movies based on it. Stoker wrote without ever visiting Romania.

I was forced at this point to leave the company of

Nikolae Paduraru, an official of the Romanian Ministry of Tourism, who was kind enough to escort me to a small island on Lake Snagov, where the real Dracula is supposedly buried. I had to follow the trail that Stoker had carved in creating the modern Western version of Dracula.

He studied the folklore of Romania and other countries where vampires were feared. His book was an artful grab bag of Middle European tales from the Dark Ages. In the aristocratic figure of Count Dracula, the deadly ghoul and accursed victim who could not die, Stoker created the first and only vampire to grip the Western imagination, the greatest fictional monster of the day. Did anything more than imagination and myth go into the creation?

It's hard to see how there could be any factual basis for the vampire legends. The superstition is so absurd physically that it seems to be an example of what Karl Marx called "the idiocy of rural life." How could vampires get in and out of their graves? How could they stay alive by imbibing blood?

Such phenomena aren't unknown to science. There are living species that habitually drink others' blood, subsisting on this alone.

There is the vampire bat, of course. This famous and hideous little mammal, *Desmodus rotundus,* is a ghost story come true. It hovers over a sleeping animal or man, alights nearby, and walks very softly so as not to awaken the sleeper. If it gets into a human's bedroom, as it sometimes does in South and Central America, it lands on the blankets, gently rears up on the tips of its wings, and crawls toward the sleeper's face. Every move is careful and stealthy.

It selects a spot for attack, a place with few nerves and plenty of blood—often an earlobe or the tip of the nose. It licks the spot, then nips the flesh gently. If the victim stirs, the vampire hops back and waits patiently until all is quiet again. Then it tests another spot.

It may try several places before finding one where the sleeper doesn't feel its nip. Then, opening its mouth wide, it makes one quick slash with its two razorlike canine teeth, sideways, as if using a knife. This makes the blood flow freely.

Vampire bats don't suck blood, they lap it up as delicately as a cat laps milk. They seem to know enough to cut a blood vessel so that the blood will keep flowing. Despite the fact that these bats feed until their bellies are bloated and they can barely fly, victims don't lose a serious amount of blood to any one bat.

Native farmers mention vampire bats as calmly as Americans mention chicken hawks. Yes, bats come at night and feed on their goats, cows, and horses. If there are many bats, sometimes the most valuable animals are taken into the huts at night, but other livestock must be risked. They seldom are harmed much. The only real danger, Indians say, is that vampires occasionally drive animals mad, making them bite everything they see. To scientists this simply means that the bats carry rabies. One outbreak spread by vampires killed off ninety percent of the cattle in some districts of southern Mexico.

When Cortez came to Mexico he found blood-sucking bats. He knew of vampire myths, so he called the creatures "vampire bats." The name stuck. Thus, nature has imitated superstition.

Vampire bats are adapted to a diet of nothing but blood. Molars, used by insect-eating bats for crushing prey, are vestigial in vampires. Their upper incisors have become long and sharp-edged, just what they need for piercing and slashing skin painlessly.

Vampire bats are never found in Europe, and myths of human vampires aren't heard where blood-drinking bats are prolific. Oceans separate the real animal and the hypothetical half human. Maybe this is because a superstition doesn't arise to account for a phenomenon easily explainable by observed natural events.

Mother Nature has also created a lesser-known creature that goes the vampire bat one better. It fastens itself on victims and sucks not only their blood but all their insides, leaving only the hollow shell of the prey's body.

This unpleasant creature wasn't discovered until 1826, on an island in the West Indies, living under rotten logs and stones and piles of damp leaves. Eventually it was found to be common in New Zealand and the center of South America—and to be incredibly ancient, the oldest "living fossil" in the world, a living link between worms and insects.

It is like a predatory snail without a shell. It is three inches long—almost precisely the same length as a vampire bat, coincidentally—with a soft body about as thick as a pencil. It has thirty-three pairs of unjointed legs, and a head crowned with two hornlike antennae.

Its discoverer, the Reverend Lansdown Guilding, gave the sluglike ravisher the name of *Peripatus,* the wandering one. He was somewhat appalled later, when he watched it feeding.

Having sighted a succulent millipede or large termite or ant, *Peripatus* extends a feathery structure that it normally keeps puckered up to hide its mouth, and fixes itself by suction to its intended victim. Using two double-bladed jaws side by side, it slices open the victim's skin and squirts a powerful sticky saliva into the wound, tenderizing the living flesh so that it can be sucked back with the saliva into the mouth. Thus it extracts a whole feast through a tiny hole.

So truth is worse than superstition, sometimes.

I found no documented records of vampirism that would impress the Society for Psychical Research. I did read a tentative explanation of the purported phenomenon, offered by some who delve into the paranormal. They say that the corporeal body is not the only body that a person possesses; he also occupies what is known as an astral body existing in a fourth or fifth dimension, seldom visible by the three-dimensional people of our sphere. When anyone dies, his astral self eventually leaves his physical husk. However, they say, in certain cases this astral body is unable to get entirely free from the physical body at the time of death. When this happens, the astral entity may roam nearby in a dreamlike state, perhaps trying to suck blood because of some perverse instinct.

However that may be, we know that certain perverse humans (alive, not returners from the grave) have done dark deeds through bloodlust or some similar urge. We think of the Marquis de Sade, of Jack the Ripper, of countless cases in Krafft-Ebing's famous collection of psychiatric case histories. We think of the chimneys of Auschwitz and the gas chambers of Belsen; of today's Manson murders and devil cults.

History records at least one authentic case of murderous craving for human blood. Elizabeth Bathory was born in 1560 at the foot of the Carpathian Mountains. She married Count Ferencz Nadasdy when she was fifteen, and moved to his remote castle. There she was initiated into peculiar rites by her manservant and an old nurse, and they began torturing servant girls in the castle. After her husband died in 1600, the countess was free to pursue her interests without restraint.

During one experiment or diversion, blood from a maid spurted onto the countess's hand. She enjoyed the sight and the sensation. She deduced that other people's blood must be good for her. Accordingly, she summoned her helpers, who cut open the maid and drained her blood into a vat. Elizabeth bathed in it, enjoyably. For ten years she continued to indulge herself in this way, using a succession of girls lured to the castle with offers of comfortable employment. But eventually an intended victim escaped and got word to the authorities.

Elizabeth's own cousin, governor of the province, led soldiers in a raid on the castle on the night of December 30, 1610. They found one girl dead and drained of blood, another alive but bleeding, and several more in the dungeon with small wounds that apparently had been inflicted for sampling purposes. Corpses of some fifty girls were found in pits below the castle.

Under house arrest, the countess was tried for murder. According to a transcript of the trial, accomplices testified against Elizabeth, but she refused to speak and there was no formal verdict against her, presumably because of her pedigree. Instead she was walled up within her bedchamber, except for a small hole through which food was passed. After four years of this confinement she died.

Seemingly Countess Elizabeth came closer to the vampirism of legend than any other known human monster. At any rate, I think she and Vlad IV were prime examples of a character trait shared by many vicious psychopaths: unlike monsters of the animal and reptile kingdoms, they had a charming side. They weren't often monstrous in their demeanor and appearance.

Elizabeth must have been regarded widely as a nice woman, else why were so many peasant girls willing to enter her service? If there were misgivings about her, how did she retain the large retinue of nonvictims needed to cook and serve and keep house?

Prince Vlad adored flowers. He endowed monasteries. He could turn a pretty girl's head. He could joke, and laugh heartily. And he was strong for civic rectitude. He maintained a sort of law and order. According to accounts in three languages, he placed a golden cup beside a fountain in Tirgoviste so that pedestrians could refresh themselves, and the cup was never stolen throughout his reign. Similarly, travelers were always said to be safe from thievery while Dracula ruled; once a stranger was robbed of 160 gold ducats, but the prince reimbursed him (and later impaled the robber).

Most evil people seem skilled in feigning goodness. There are many reports of smiling monsters who enticed their victims into captivity and torture. Maybe some monsters had a truly good side.

Badness among humans is only a question of degree. Corrupted by power, any of us might conceivably become monstrous. Machiavelli wrote that all men are naturally bad. Joseph Conrad put it more precisely: "The belief in a supernatural source of evil is not necessary; men alone are quite capable of every wickedness."

Would Conrad, I wondered, have carried his argument to the point of asserting that we could believe in vampires (or at least in blood-sucking human predators) without believing in the supernatural?

Perhaps. Nature has created many things besides

vampire bats and slugs that instinctively crave the blood of other living creatures. We think of mosquitoes and fleas. We think of a leech that sucks the blood of a horse or sucks empty a whole snail with equal gusto. We think of the sea lampreys that squirm their way into the Great Lakes, where they attach themselves to migrating salmon and suck their blood.

When I looked into the subject, I found that a vampirelike, parasitic way of life has been adopted by an extraordinary assortment of organisms—including representatives of almost every major group of microbes, plants, and animals. All viruses are parasites, and many kinds of protozoa and bacteria have turned into parasites. There are rapacious plunderers among the higher plants—mistletoe and dodder and the strangler fig, for example. On a smaller scale, every species of flowering plant is exploited by insects, nematodes, and fungi that dig into its tissues, then live by sucking it.

A mammal can support a whole menagerie of creatures feasting on its blood or flesh: ticks and mites and flies on the outside, worms in the liver and lungs and intestines, protozoa in the blood. They can taint their chosen prey with malaria, sleeping sickness, yellow fever, and other diseases.

A tapeworm several yards long will live comfortably inside a man. This pale, blind devourer is an unpleasant guest. Its head is tiny, with barely a speck of a brain. But the head carries suckers that will fasten it to the intestinal wall. The tapeworm needs neither mouth nor gut because its food is digested for it by the human host; it can cheat the host of nourishing fluids by absorbing them through the surface of its body. Human digestive juices, which destroy other substances in the intestine, are powerless against the tapeworm.

Other creatures may live independently, foraging for themselves, or may turn parasitic and thereupon transform themselves so phenomenally that only a specialist would recognize them as the free-living things they once were. For example, there are species of crustaceans, usually eaten by fish, that turn the tables and settle down as parasites on fishes' gills or skin. Then they change into something very like blind worms. Never to swim or crawl again, they let themselves be carried about by the fish, so their lively legs and segmented shells drop away, and their jaws change into suckers with which they extract body fluids from the host. These tiny monsters shed their sense organs, even their eyes, because these organs become needless. Gorging themselves continuously, they grow far fatter than their independent brethren.

So we can't say that a vampire's way of life is alien to nature. There's nothing supernatural or paranormal about it. However, among humans a vampire might be so unnatural as to be impossible—or would it?

I came across Charles Fort's book *Wild Talents,* in which he cited four disconcertingly relevant news stories.

In 1867 the captain of a fishing smack outside Boston noticed that two crewman were missing, and went below to seek them. In the dark hold he lifted his lantern and saw one of the men in the arms of a Portuguese sailor who called himself James Brown. Brown's mouth was on the man's throat, sucking blood. The body of the other missing sailor lay nearby; it apparently was bloodless. "Brown" was tried, convicted, and sentenced to be hanged, but an incredulous President Andrew Johnson commuted his sentence to life imprisonment. Twenty-five years later this putative vampire was transferred from the Ohio Penitentiary to the National Asylum in Washington, D.C., and his story was retold in the Brooklyn *Eagle* for November 4, 1892.

On September 17, 1910, a child was found dead in a field near the town of Galazanna, Portugal. The body seemed drained of blood, though very little blood was visible around it. The child had last been seen with a man named Salvarrey. He was arrested, and confessed that he was a vampire.

On December 29, 1913, a woman known as "Scotch Dolly" was found battered and dead in her room at 18 Etham Street, S.E., London. An inquest rendered a verdict of death from heart failure and shock. However, on one of her legs were thirty-eight little double wounds. The coroner asked, "Have you ever had a similar case?" The doctor who performed the autopsy answered, "No, not exactly like this."

In 1929 the people of Düsseldorf, Germany, were terrified by the similar murders of eight women and a man. Peter Kurten was caught and tried for the killings. He made no defense, but described himself as a vampire. The New York *Sun* for April 14, 1931, tells the story in detail.

These cases sound to us like grotesqueries. They might have sounded otherwise to various ethnic groups that often ate human flesh and drank human fluids, ostensibly in order to enhance their own strength, courage, or vitality. Chinese peasants sucked the bile of bandits they executed, according to *The Golden Bough;* Celebes headhunters quaffed the blood and spooned up the brains of their victims; the Nauras Indians of New Granada munched the hearts of captured Spaniards; the Italones of the Philippines ate enemies' entrails raw; the notorious Zulu chief Matuana drank the gall of thirty captured rival chieftains; mountain tribes in southeast Africa held initiation rites in which they fed young men a paste made of human testicles, human livers, ground-up human ears, and skin. When Sir Charles McCarthy was killed by the Ashantis in 1824, it was said that their chiefs shared morsels of his heart and flesh at a victory banquet.

Such dietary quirks might be highly nutritious, for all we know. Human blood contains carbohydrates, vitamins, minerals, and amino acids. Other organs contain other health-giving substances. We customarily cut these organs out of various animals and devour them.

So perhaps a human "vampire" needn't be thought so unnatural after all. Local customs and individual preferences could make quite a difference.

What of that other supposedly occult aberration, lycanthropy?

Belief in it used to be widespread, and I was told that countless families in the Balkans still believe.

Among modern psychiatrists, "lycanthropy" is a standard term for a peculiarly hideous state of mind. Dictionaries and encyclopedias define it in such terms as these: "A kind of insanity in which the patient imagines himself to be a wolf or other wild beast, and exhibits the tastes, voice, etc. of that animal. . . . A morbid desire for eating human flesh appears in certain extreme cases."

The Jungian psychologist Robert Eisler wrote a classic study, *Man Into Wolf,* in 1949. He argued that primitive man naturally picked up ferocity and blood-lust from the wild animals that threatened him daily, and that this same proclivity may sleep deep within the psyche of modern man, an atavism that still can emerge if roused.

Eisler's theory could explain the cults of leopard-men and hyena-men with their bestial dances and rituals in African jungles—and not always just in the jungles. According to William Seabrook, a quiet little native clerk in one African town donned a panther skin with sharp claws and killed a girl. The clerk was totally convinced that he became a panther periodically, and told Seabrook that he much preferred panther ways to human ways.

Seabrook also reported a case of a Russian immigrant woman in New York, meditating on the mystical *I Ching*'s hexagram 49, which is associated with animal fur. She imagined that she was a wolf in the snow, and began to bay, then slaver. Someone tried to bring her out of the dream or trance, whereupon she sprang at his throat.

There are records of a certain Gilles Garnier, executed in France in 1574. The charge alleged that he seized a half-grown girl, killed her in a vineyard with his teeth and hands, then dragged her with his teeth into the woods at La Serre, where he ate most of her. He admitted that he had previously strangled a ten-year-old boy and chewed off a leg, and mangled a small girl but fled when interrupted.

Sex killers in our own day have been known to dine on a victim's flesh. Albert Fish cooked and ate tender parts of a ten-year-old girl, Grace Budd, at Greenport, New York, in 1928. A Wisconsin tailor named Edmund Gein ate uncooked portions of women he slew, and made vests for himself from their skin. This brings to mind the fertility rites of Aztec priests who flayed virgins and dressed in their bloody skins to perform a sacred dance.

Folklore of many lands agreed that men might become animals. Pausanius recorded that Arcadian Greece was troubled by citizens who actually ran with the wolves. Ovid told of Lycaon, king of Arcadia, who served "hash of human flesh" at his banquet tables, and eventually turned into a wolf. Legend said that Vereticus, king of Wales, was transformed into a wolf by the punitory Saint Patrick. (For a long time afterward, Wales paid a yearly tribute of three hundred wolves to British kings.) The Neuri people assumed the shape of wolves at will, according to Herodotus; so did the family of Antaeus, Pliny said, and they chose one of their number by lot each year to turn wolf.

Sir James Frazer, one of the greatest authorities on the folklore of magic, tells in *The Golden Bough* of presumed tiger-men, cat-men, and even crocodile-men in China, adding that each part of the world had its own variations on this theme. To most believers the transformation into a beast wasn't just a figure of speech or a delusion; it was an actual metamorphosis.

Souls of the dead were believed to return occasionally, either in bodily form or in the guise of animals. Even the souls of the living were supposed to be able to leave their bodies and lead a semiindependent part-time existence, perhaps by taking nonhuman shape. Sometimes the metamorphosis was involuntary, people said; it might be a punishment from heaven, or a spell cast by an enemy skilled in black arts.

As I traveled back toward the modern world, I learned that belief in werewolves was still strong in the darker corners of Transylvania and Walachia. I also learned (from libraries, later) that the term *werewolf* doesn't denote an ex-wolf. It comes from the old Germanic word *wer,* which comes from the Roman *vir,* both meaning man—so that werewolf is the name for a man-wolf.

During Dracula's lifetime an international council of theologians, convoked by King Sigismund of Hungary and Bohemia, studied certain data and decided that the werewolf was a real and present danger. It had the appetite of a wolf, they agreed, and prowled at night, devouring children, ravishing flocks and herds, sometimes digging up corpses. But they couldn't agree on whether it took the visible shape of the beast it emulated.

There was and is less uncertainty about werewolves among the unschooled. Their tales seem to prove the physical reality of such incarnations. One element is common to most of these tales: someone attacked by a werewolf manages to wound it; later a man or woman is found with a very similar wound, and confesses to being the werewolf. What could be more damning? they ask.

Frazer tells of a huntsman in the Auvergne who hacked off the paw of a wolf that charged him, and kept the paw as a trophy. Later he found it to be a woman's hand, with a ring on the finger, which was recognized as belonging to a well-known lady of the town. The lady, nursing a wrist from which the hand had been severed, confessed to lycanthropy, and was burned.

Olaus Magnus, a medieval chronicler, wrote a report of a slave who sought to convince his mistress that werewolves existed, and therefore came bounding out of her cellar in the form of a wolf; attacked by her dogs, he lost an eye. The next day the slave was found lacking an eye.

The most detailed werewolf report that I have read is in London's *Cornhill Magazine* for October 1918. An article by Richard Bagot concerning things he saw and heard in northern Nigeria recounts an experience with raiding hyenas. The beasts were wounded by gun traps. Their bloody trail was followed to a point where the hyena tracks ended and were succeeded by human footprints, leading to a native village.

Bagot also quoted a story by a Captain Shott, who alleged that he had shot away the jaw of an "enormous brute" of some kind. He pursued the wounded animal, only to find that the tracks led into a town. A native died there the next day. His jaw had been torn off.

I went home wondering. Such stories were hardly credible. Assuming them to be false, could we then say that a metamorphosed human beast is only a figment of superstition? According to psychologists, it comes out of our subconscious, which seems to be populated with monsters that appear normal enough and yet terrify us. They are the predators we occasionally meet in a nightmare, huge animals with slavering jaws and glowing eyes who nonetheless act peacefully for the time being. The theory is that such dream creatures are projections of whatever traits are most threatening in ourselves— dangerous desires disguised as beasts.

Transformation of man into beast would seem physically impossible. One might also think it physically impossible for a fish to turn into a frog.

But that is what the tadpole does. Its gills disappear; its tail goes back into its body somehow; legs sprout; the tiny mouth widens fantastically; the eyes bulge larger and larger. Finally we see a rebuilt creature, sitting on dry land instead of swimming under water.

The tadpole-frog is one of a legion of creatures endowed with the power (or the destiny, I suppose) to transform themselves. A certain cicada burrows into damp soil to dwell for seventeen years, then crawls out as the famous "seventeen-year locust" that ravages crops. A fat caterpillar stops and spins a silky shroud; apparently dead as a mummy, he soon is reincarnated as a gorgeous winged moth or butterfly.

Internally as well as externally, some creatures undergo total change. Inside a caterpillar-butterfly pupa, organs crumble like crackers crushed into soup. Disarrayed cells are reassembled at different locations, where they coalesce into new organs. Entire new sensory systems sprout. We would call this magic if we didn't know better.

Even in maturity, a few animals make seemingly

magical changes that humans apparently cannot. A star-fish produces new parts if some are damaged. Newts and salamanders promptly replace lost limbs by growing new ones. Lizards regrow lost tails.

In the plant kingdom there are wild transformations if special events call them forth. A plant shorn of leaves by some disaster often makes new ones in unexpected places; trees generate leaves on their trunks, for instance. Roots don't normally grow out of leaves, but you can push an African violet leaf into a pot and it will make new roots and a new young plant. A begonia leaf in contact with soil will turn its ribs into roots. Branches of the tropical gumbo limbo tree are widely used for fence posts; soon these posts take root and sprout leaves, and in a few years the fence turns into a line of trees.

You can't always predict what a creature will turn into, even if you know the life history of others that look virtually identical. An underwater larva indistin-guishable from many others will grow legs, then eat and digest its own skin, and emerge as a red salamander. Tiny plankton organisms in the ocean turn into jellyfish, snails, clams, octopuses, oysters, or sea urchins, as dictated by the blueprints of their genes.

Can genes go awry in higher species? Well, we know what cancer can do. We know of two-headed calves, of human freaks in sideshows, of baby monstrosities born to mothers who took Thalidomide.

But can genes go so far awry as to turn a man into a wolf or hyena or a blood-sucking parasite? Surely not.

Well, almost surely not.

12

Monsters from the Laboratory

One night in 1816 a nineteen-year-old girl conjured up
a dim shape from some dark maze of myth and imagination. She called it merely "the monster" or sometimes
"the daemon." Soon it was famous.

It even took on a kind of immortality, becoming one
of the best-known and most terrifying of all imaginary
monsters. Scholars have long wondered where she
really got the idea for it, and what the factual basis for
it, if any, might have been.

Her monster was a man-thing, made of corpses from
churchyards and hospitals, galvanized into life by an
electric shock. Soon it turned against the experimenter
who invented it, and destroyed him.

In recent years this monster has grown more frightening than it used to be—for it now looks more like fact
than fiction. Science has invented techniques for creating living things—even pseudohuman things—and is
using those techniques, although many prominent scientists have campaigned passionately to outlaw them.

The girl who thought up the prototype of laboratory-
made monsters was born Mary Godwin. She called herself Mary Wollstonecraft, after her mother, who had
been one of England's most liberated feminists. The
mother died soon after giving birth to Mary, and the
girl often sat for hours by her mother's gravestone, writ-
ing or reading.

The idea of a man-made monster came to her during

a strange hectic summer at Lake Geneva. She was there with a married man, the famous poet Percy Bysshe Shelley, whom she had met at her father's house. (Her father was William Godwin, an optimistic radical who saw no need for law or institutions.)

In Geneva, Shelley and Mary struck up a friendship with another famed young poet, Lord George Gordon Byron. Scandal had made him a social outcast from England. He had deserted his wife; made love to his half-sister; emulated the "vampires" of folklore by residing in an abandoned (and supposedly haunted) abbey; killed his Turkish mistress, rumor said, by drowning her in a sack; and now feared that his past had brought down a curse that would destroy him and his friends. In Geneva he was surrounded by a retinue of servants as well as a young girl who had wooed him by mail, and a jealous personal physician.

The poets and assorted camp followers moved into adjoining villas on the lake. The weather was hot and gloomy. There were squalls, gusting winds, and violent thunder and lightning. Some astronomers and other seers, descrying mysterious spots on the sun, said that the world might end that summer. The Swiss authorities warned people to stay indoors.

On the evening of June 16 a storm raged. Both households were pent up in Byron's villa, and tempers smoldered. Several amorous triangles had generated jealousies and intrigues. For diversion, Byron read several creepy tales aloud to the group, and finally proposed that everyone go somewhere alone and write a horror story.

Of them all, only Mary Wollstonecraft Godwin's tale, *Frankenstein,* turned out to be noteworthy—so noteworthy, in fact, that its name is still known the world around. It has been translated into every major language, republished countless times in hard-cover and paperback, and transferred onto the stage and screen.

There is a common misconception that Frankenstein is the monster. This blunder has won wide acceptance through long circulation. Even the erudite *The New*

York Times misused the name at least once: "One would like to know what would have happened had the politicians not created a Frankenstein."

Even people who are aware that the creator-victim of the monster was Frankenstein are still likely to call him "Doctor" Frankenstein—another mistake. (The *Harper Dictionary of Contemporary Usage* says, wrongly, "Frankenstein was a doctor, the protagonist of a book of the same name, who created a monster that got out of control and destroyed the doctor.") He wasn't a doctor; he wasn't even a medical student.

Victor Frankenstein, according to the novel, was a seventeen-year-old student of natural history at the University of Ingolstadt, where he fabricated his man-thing. There really was an Ingolstadt in Bavaria, and it had a university. There also was a Castle Frankenstein; Mary and Shelley may have visited it on their way through the Rhineland. If so, she probably heard legends of Johann Konrad Dippel, a noted alchemist who was born in the castle and grew up as a servant there in the early eighteenth century. Dippel eventually won a reputation as a "miracle worker" through cures he wrought with a secret formula; he tried unsuccessfully to barter the secret for title to Castle Frankenstein.

Modern researchers, perhaps fancifully, hint that Dippel might have wanted to use the secluded castle for sinister experiments in creating immortal forms of human life. He did announce, in a pamphlet printed in 1733, that his hidden skill would keep him alive until the year 1801. He was found dead of unknown causes in 1734.

Frankenstein's author never said much about where she got the name for her novel or the idea for her monster. She did hint, in an introduction to the book, at a nightmare brought on by tense scenes in Byron's villa and the shocks of a Genevan thunderstorm. She wrote:

Successive images arose in my mind with a vividness far beyond the usual bounds. I saw the pale student of unhallowed arts kneeling beside the thing he had put together. I saw the hideous phantasm . . . show signs of life, and stir with an uneasy, half-vital motion.

Long afterward, an English literary critic tried to sum up what had happened with an offhand remark: "That poor girl, driven almost mad by Shelley's drivelling conversation, wrote *Frankenstein*." Her fantasy did seem horribly half mad to many readers and perhaps to the author herself. It certainly wasn't an attempt at science fiction.

Her bent was literary, not medical or biological. She may have known the Greek legend of Pygmalion, a sculptor who fell in love with a statue he had created, and was enabled by the gods to bring it to life. Or she may have heard of the Golem (a Hebrew word meaning something embryonic or incompletely formed) in medieval Jewish legends; it was a zombielike servant made of clay and given life by means of a charm. Golem had been attributed to several rabbis in different European countries; the most famous legend told of a rabbi in sixteenth-century Prague who made a Golem but was forced to destroy it after it ran amok.

There was nothing in Mary's novel hinting at how an artificial man might be created. She glossed over the process with a few vague sentences. She didn't mention recent work by the Italian anatomist Luigi Galvani, who discovered that the muscles of dissected frogs would clench and jump if simultaneously touched by two different metals (thus adding the word *galvanize* to the English language), or the work by Sir Humphry Davy in using electricity to pull apart the atoms of tightly bound molecules, thus pointing the way to the remaking of living tissue.

Although Mary evidently had no inkling of it, many scientists were groping toward knowledge that could make her nightmare-novel come true. For example, they already knew that certain simple living creatures, when badly mutilated, could regrow into entire organisms, a process called "regeneration."

The more primitive the creature, the more miraculously it put itself back together. Very primitive animals like sponges were squeezed through a silk cloth and broken down to their individual cells; the cells then regrouped into an intact creature. Slightly higher up the evolutionary scale, a hydra could survive beheading; when decapitated, it simply grew a new head, and when chopped into pieces, each piece grew into a complete organism. Lizards, salamanders, and newts were seen to grow new tails and legs, and even as much as half of a heart. Sailors discovered that an octopus would grow new tentacles to replace any they cut off. Why shouldn't mankind do as well or better? This question fascinated many biologists.

But they were not to approach the fictitious feat of Victor Frankenstein for many decades yet. The how and why of regeneration continued to baffle researchers. What was the electrical signal or chemical change that started the process? Why were mammals, man included, incapable of regenerating more than a bit of bone? (We regrow a lost toenail, but not a lost toe.) Because scientists couldn't experiment on human beings—that privilege was reserved for doctors and druggists—they kept making various tests with other creatures.

For example, they dabbled in "mutations"—that is, freak animals, or monsters, which the ancients had regarded as bad omens. They grew interested in the feat of a Massachusetts farmer named Seth Wright, who in 1791 had disregarded superstition and gone ahead to breed freaks, after a lamb on his farm was born with abnormally short legs. This shrewd New Englander realized that short-legged animals couldn't escape over the low stone walls around his farm. So he deliberately mated other sheep with the stunted one, and grew richer by producing a flock of short-legged sheep. This proved that animals could be bred with almost any characteristics their human creator chose. Frankenstein had never aspired to such skill.

The freak sheep inspired many experimenters to seek profitable mutations. By the end of the nineteenth century a great horticulturist, Luther Burbank, was breeding hundreds of new varieties of plants, not only by mutations but by judicious crossing and grafting. Meanwhile, biologists working with fruit flies discovered a way to cause frequent and bizarre mutations, in order to study the inheritance of such changes: they exposed the flies to X-rays or microwaves. They were learning how to control genes.

The flies gave military men food for thought. In 1763 a British general decimated potentially bothersome Indian tribes in the Ohio Valley by giving them blankets contaminated with smallpox. Flies and other insects could carry diseases; perhaps laboratory-bred insects, or even bacteria, could be given deadly plagues to unleash on an enemy. Laboratories got busy stockpiling tiny living monsters for chemical and biological warfare.

The stockpiles have apparently been destroyed now, or sealed up, because national governments as well as scientists renounced these forms of warfare when they realized that the creators themselves could be plagued by what they created. However, experimenters kept designing microbes for useful purposes, without much thought about what might happen if an experiment went wrong.

One laboratory developed four strains of bacteria that "ate" petroleum, converting it into protein, carbon dioxide, and water. The trouble was that each of these strains attacked only a few of the many different hydrocarbons in oil, and each worked too slowly to be useful in cleaning up massive oil spills. But in 1975 a microbiologist at General Electric announced that he had combined the oil-consuming capacities of the various strains into a superbug. This hybrid showed an undiscriminating appetite for all hydrocarbons and phenomenal speed in devouring them. General Electric proclaimed this work "the first successful application of advanced genetic engineering techniques." The chief technique used was irradiating the bacteria with ultraviolet light, which fused genetic material.

But what would happen if such mutant microbes developed unexpected traits, as mosquitoes did when they developed immunity to DDT or as the malaria parasite did in becoming resistant to new "wonder drug" antibiotics? Nobody knew. And the question didn't seem important. The oil-devourers were benign bacteria. Except for one point, all would be well. The bacteria unleashed in scooping up an oil spill would have to find more sustenance. They might well be forced to devour subsurface oil reserves.

Obviously, ominous things can happen in laboratories. There was the sinister metamorphosis of a blood-sucking insect called a Rhodnius. If left to itself, it stayed a small insect. But the British zoologist V. B. Wigglesworth, who has spent a lifetime studying metamorphosis, discovered that when he cut off this evil insect's head, the body not only stayed alive—as the hydra does—but became a giant new insect.

Dr. Wigglesworth found that the head contained a hormone that stopped the insect's growth at a pre-ordained time; without the head, body growth could continue unchecked. Suppose some of these decapitated insects escaped and began breeding? Or suppose some other creature happened to lose a head, with equally unexpected results? Conceivably we could see throwbacks to the earth's Carboniferous period, about two hundred million years ago, when insects had three-foot wing spans. The thought of yardstick-size hornets, mosquitoes, locusts, and other noxious insects is more nightmarish to some than the thought of Frankenstein's soulless man-monster.

Dangerous organisms have been known to escape from top laboratories. Cultures of live smallpox virus—bottled plague, so to speak—are kept at nine research laboratories in the United States and at an unknown number of places elsewhere, so that scientists can make comparative tests in cases of a future pox-virus outbreak. In 1973, through a combination of minor laxities, the virus infected a new lab technician at the London School of Tropical Medicine; she didn't even know the virus was there. Eleven days later she fell ill, and lay in an open ward of a hospital for a week before anyone suspected infectious smallpox. Two deaths resulted. A smallpox scare swept London. Millions of pounds were spent tracing suspected carriers and vaccinating them.

Only luck averted a devastating epidemic. Since then, many laboratories have tightened their security—but who can be sure that security will always stay tight enough?

Since 1931 scientists have known that some forty diseases are caused by viruses, but at that time they didn't know what viruses were. Finally an English bacteriologist trapped some in filters and proved, at least, that they were material particles of some kind. Were they living or dead particles? Their power to multiply and to transmit disease certainly hinted that they were alive. But an American biochemist, Wendell Stanley, won a Nobel Prize for isolating a virus in crystalline form. The fact that viruses could be crystallized seemed to prove that they were merely dead protein; nothing living had ever been crystallized. A crystal is geometric and solid, like an emerald; how could it live? Yet the fact remained that viruses could reproduce, could infect animals and people with disease even after having been crystallized. How could any dead thing spawn others like itself?

Eventually all viruses proved to be nucleoprotein, composed of the same stuff as genes—which are the very essence of life. Viruses still don't fit any standard definition of either "animate" or "inanimate." They are the ultimate parasites, because they are the smallest creatures that attack cells, yet they are among the most fierce.

We can picture viruses in the cell as vampire raiders who push aside the supervising genes and reduce a healthy, productive cell to a mere nursery that fosters a new generation of viruses. The infected cell stops producing its own hereditary material, and begins manufacturing the malign viruses instead. After twenty minutes or so, the cell may die and burst, releasing as many as three hundred full-grown new viruses to pry their way into other cells. The body responds to these living-dead newcomers as it does to germs: it makes antibodies. The war between the antibodies and the viruses determines whether the host animal lives or dies.

By 1960 virologists were actually taking viruses apart

and putting them together again. A German-American biochemist, Heinz Fraenkel-Conrat, separated the nucleic acid and protein portions of a virus and tried to find out whether either alone could infect a cell. Separately they couldn't. But when he mixed the protein and nucleic acid together again, much of the original virulence of the virus was restored!

The separated substances had seemed dead. They came to life when he combined them. Although the press announced that Fraenkel-Conrat had created life from dead substances, later experiments proved that the life was already there, in the nucleic acid.

Viruses are man's most monstrous living enemy, except man himself. They are all but invulnerable to attack by drugs or any other artificial weapon. Only the body's natural defenses have a chance to defeat them. You might think that further research into the mysterious ways of our formidable little foe would be encouraged everywhere. Until 1972 it was. But in the autumn of that year a biologist named Robert Pollack began telephoning other biologists all over the country, trying to drum up an emergency meeting.

Pollack had been intensely aroused by an argument he had had with an advanced student in a summer class Pollack taught at Cold Spring Harbor Laboratory in New York. "I chose to talk about the safety and ethics of working with biological materials," he explained. "I talked about how to keep from getting contaminated. Then I talked about the danger of doing something that might screw things up in a much larger way. I got a lot of argument, in particular by one girl from Paul Berg's lab at Stanford. She said they were joining the genetic blueprint of a virus called SV40 with part of the genetic instructions in a bacterial virus called phage lambda, and then were putting the combination into *Escherichia coli* bacteria.

"I had a fit. SV40 is a virus that causes cancer in mice. In tissue cultures in the lab, it also transforms individual human cells. Bacteriophage lambda just naturally lives in *E. coli*, which is a bug that just naturally lives in people's guts. So the cancer virus would be offered a route into human cells that never occurs in nature. I called up Berg. . . . He said, 'Let me think about your objections.' "

Berg recalled later, "When Bob called I was frankly quite upset. I felt that most of the dangers were remote. But the more I thought about it, the more I found I was persuading myself. I don't see this as a great moral or ethical issue; I see it more as a problem of public health. So we turned that experiment off."

Stanford's scientists had gone further than anyone else in genetic engineering. Before they learned how, no two species could interbreed to produce fertile offspring. There was no way for any horse gene to be introduced into a cow, for example. So the genetic cards couldn't be reshuffled much. Then scientists at Stanford broke the species barrier—in one sector, at least. Nobody has yet interbred cattle and horses, but Stanford accomplished one-way genetic exchange between certain kinds of microbes and almost any other living creature, including man.

All the experiments performed—and planned—involved the *E. coli*, because it is by far the best-understood microbe and because it multiplies readily in laboratories. But *E. coli* microbes thrive in a wide range of places, including the place they're named for, the human colon.

This was what frightened Pollack. Suppose the mutant *E. coli*, laden with cancer virus, crawled out of the lab, and suppose someone swallowed a few of them. They would move happily into their natural habitat, a human intestinal tract. There they might create a new kind of cancer. Or they might make a dangerous toxin. Or they might repel a curative antibiotic.

All these mights changed Berg's mind. He offered to help organize the meeting Pollack had proposed.

So a hundred biologists met in California in January 1973. They talked for three days about "such things as wild viruses from experimental monkeys, or exotic virus-caused dementias, or cancer viruses contaminating the cultures in which polio vaccines are made, or virus hybrids created in the laboratory," as a researcher later recalled.

The conferees agreed informally to stop playing God with genetic codes until they found safer ways to do it. But they had no authority to shut down anyone else's research program. As alarm spread, a group of scientists asked the National Academy of Sciences to appoint a study committee.

The committee was duly formed, with Berg as chairman, and convened in April 1974 at Massachusetts Institute of Technology. Berg went there already convinced that risks were mounting. His post at Stanford, where some of the newest research was progressing, gave him a unique overview of the situation.

"Nobody else knew," he said later, "of the pressure from people calling us daily wanting materials to do similar experiments. Some of them had horror experiments planned. At MIT, within one hour we agreed that an international conference in 1975 would be our first recommendation. But we realized that if we waited for the big meeting, most of the molecules that we were worried about would already have been made. So we appealed for an immediate suspension of work."

Eleven prominent molecular biologists wrote an open letter asking their colleagues throughout the world to postpone all further work along certain specified lines. Their unprecedented letter was endorsed by the National Academy of Science, and was published in two distinguished scientific weeklies, the American *Science* and the British *Nature*. Most of the signatories had been doing the very work they now warned against, transplanting into bacteria genes from cancer-causing or other kinds of viruses, and genes that would help the bacteria resist drugs.

Many scientists who abided by the requested ban nevertheless chafed. They saw it as a needless restraint on their freedom to pursue whatever lines of inquiry they chose. So they waited impatiently for a showdown.

Inevitably, the showdown came at the big conference in February 1975 at Asilomar, California. There were

146 participants—one-third more than expected. Scientists came from the Soviet Union, Japan, Israel, Australia, and ten European countries. Fierce arguments broke out immediately.

The fireworks were touched off by the famous American biochemist James D. Watson, Nobel Prize winner for his work on the structure of the DNA molecule that stores the information of heredity and makes copies of it during cell division. Watson shocked some of his friends by publicly changing sides. He was one of the eleven who had signed the original call for deferral of research. But now he demanded that the ban be lifted.

"I thought we should have six months to see if anything would frighten us," he told the conference. "The dangers are probably no greater than working in a hospital. You can't measure the risk. They want to put people out of business for something you can't measure."

A directly opposite point of view was put forward by Sidney Brenner, an eminent British geneticist. He warned, "The immediate risks are of course to the scientists, but they are also to the innocent within institutions that practice science—technicians, students, sweepers. You've got to make sure that people who don't know they're taking the risk are exposed as little as possible."

Outside the meeting, Brenner told reporters that he was shocked by American biologists' obsession with narrow interests. "I kept hearing the word *business,*" he said, "as in 'You'll put me out of business with these restrictions.' Many times."

In the heat of discussion a brilliant idea bubbled up: why not breed a new strain of "disabled" microbes that would die if they strayed from their laboratory cradles? Biologists and geneticists could then experiment with these microbes to their hearts' content. A committee worked through the night preparing, duplicating, and stapling a statement to be laid before the conference the next morning.

The statement suggested that low-risk experiments be resumed, under the normal precautions taken in handling dangerous viruses. But moderate-risk and high-risk experiments would still be banned until the safe experimental bacteria were bred. This statement carried overwhelmingly, with no more than five or six votes against any section.

"Most of the scientists, from many countries, had said little or nothing, but listened," Brenner said afterward. "In the end it was they, the silent majority, who brought it together."

Developing a bacterium that was sickly enough took longer than expected. Roy Curtiss of the University of Alabama Medical Center, who had originally proposed the idea, volunteered to do the job. He set out to develop a strain of *E. coli* that would be addicted to special food provided in the lab. But each time he caused a mutation, the new strain showed a surprising ability to adjust to the hardships he thought would be fatal. However, in fourteen months the sickliest, feeblest microbe on the face of the earth was available for experimenters. Several large freezers in Birmingham are now stocked with rack upon rack of test tubes containing these pampered creatures and their nutrient. If they should ever escape from a tube, ordinary sunlight might kill them before they die of starvation or pop their skin. (Curtiss has created a hybrid that lacks the normal tough outer coat.)

In April 1976 a National Institute of Health committee, charged with protecting the public's safety, officially certified the new strain (named $x1776$) for use in experiments. The age of genetic engineering, with its immense promise, is now safely under way. Since cancer is a fundamental disruption of controlled cell growth, genetic engineering can be said to offer hope for a cancer cure. And of course it may eventually enable man to overcome birth defects or any other innate weaknesses.

On the other hand, live plants and animals are now being made to order. And this may pose other perils.

WE HAVE THE AWFUL KNOWLEDGE TO MAKE EXACT COPIES OF HUMAN BEINGS, warned a headline in the sober, precise *New York Times* for March 5, 1972. It added in smaller heading, *The Frankenstein myth becomes a reality*.

The author of the *Times* article, Professor Willard

Gaylin, M.D., declared in his first paragraph, "The people are shielded, by the complexity of genetic science, from an understanding of the nature and magnitude of threats it poses to their ways of life and their very existence as a species."

Other scientists sounded just as grim. "We may be on the brink of a major evolutionary perturbation," said Joshua Lederberg, a very senior biologist from Stanford. Robert Sinsheimer, chairman of the biology department at California Institute of Technology, put it more strongly: "I think the potential exists for some kind of biological catastrophe." In England, the Medical Research Council requested British laboratories to stop "further research with human embryos."

What were all these scientists so exercised about?

They saw strange visions of living creatures, shaped more or less like man, that might be bred in test tubes. The creatures could be supermen or monsters. They could be born with six arms if a scientist-creator chose. They could be ready-made giants or dwarfs. They could be the identical twins of any specified human being—or triplets, quadruplets, or more. The labs should be able to copy off unlimited numbers of parahuman entities, all precisely alike.

Mary Wollstonecraft's nightmare vision, multiplied to infinity, now seems close to coming true. Biologists learned to grow entire living things more than a decade ago. A headline in the Los Angeles *Times* for November 2, 1964, announced: EXPERTS SAY MAN MAY REPRODUCE LIKE PLANTS.

Horticulturists have long been able to take a "cutting" from a plant and grow a replica of the original plant. With similar techniques, could a snippet of tissue from a human be made to duplicate that human? Apparently it could. The first big step toward this came when F. C. Steward, a cellular physiologist at Cornell, took individual cells from a carrot root—the part we eat—and bathed them in coconut milk and other nutrients. "We were hardly prepared for the dramatic effects," he wrote. "It was as if the cell's idling engine of growth had been put in gear." In three weeks the tissue multiplied about eightyfold.

Steward tried other growth-stimulating substances on the carrot tissue, and learned how to persuade individual root cells to form clumps. Some grew to giant size. Some formed filaments. Some made buds. Most amazing of all, some clumps put out roots. At last Steward coaxed an individual cell to the ultimate stage of a full-grown carrot plant—roots, stalk, leaves, flowers, seeds, and all.

Later experiments showed that any plant cell, suitably encouraged, might grow into a full plant. The big question, of course, was whether such a genetic explosion was possible with animal cells.

Again the answer proved to be yes. John B. Gurdon, a cell biologist at Oxford, learned how to make numerous live identical copies of one frog. He proved that a specialized intestinal cell from the frog contained the full library of genetic instructions needed to build a tadpole. The resulting infant had only one parent: the frog from which the intestinal cell was taken. And the infant was identical with this parent, just as if they were identical twins. Tadpoles thus produced became frogs and reproduced normally, despite their peculiar heritage.

The procedure for duplicating a frog or carrot was called cloning, from a Greek word meaning "sprout" or "throng," and the resulting facsimile became known as a clone.

Cloning offers the potential, immediately, of producing exact copies of prize bulls, pedigreed dogs, or exceptional human beings. So far no one is known to have done this—partly because the cellular manipulations involved would be far more difficult than in simple small creatures like frogs. But there are eminent scientists who see it coming soon.

Professor J. B. S. Haldane, one of the most brilliant and practical scientists of our time, predicted a few years ago that "we may find out at any moment" how to clone people. Joshua Lederberg said, "It wouldn't surprise me if it comes any day now. When someone will try it in a man, I haven't the foggiest idea. Anywhere within fifteen years."

"All smaller countries possess the resources required," wrote Professor Watson in a 1976 article. "A human being born of clonal reproduction most likely will appear within twenty to fifty years, and even sooner if some nation should actively promote the venture."

In other words, if a Third World dictator, for example, should decide to mass-produce tougher soldiers, smarter scientists, more-energetic workmen, or more-fertile women, he might pour the necessary resources into perfecting the techniques, and put them into operation secretly. Western civilizations might then face a dilemma of either competing or surrendering.

An entirely different laboratory procedure, also known for years, offers another alternative to normal sexual reproduction. When an egg cell is stimulated mechanically or chemically, it starts the growth that leads to birth even though it is unfertilized. This virgin birth, or parthenogenesis, occurs in nature. Bees do it, some birds do it, certain fleas do it. Virgin births of turkeys have been observed.

Artificial parthenogenesis was attempted in laboratories as long ago as 1900. Today, high-school biology students know that unfertilized frog eggs, pricked with a pin, hatch normal tadpoles. On a more sophisticated scale, researchers have found that mouse eggs, shocked by electricity or dunked in a salty liquid, become self-fertilized. A whole rabbit has been hatched from an unfertilized egg, according to the *New York Times*.

However, a creature formed by virgin birth isn't genetically identical with its mother, or with anything. The hazard of creating abnormal human children this way haunts many scientists. "I wouldn't want to implant an embryo unless I had the right to terminate a monster which developed out of it," Watson said.

It was John Gurdon who merged parthenogenesis with cloning. Working with a frog's fertilized egg, he lifted out the nucleus (which holds almost all the genetic information) and replaced it with a nucleus drawn from an ordinary body cell of a tadpole of the same species. The egg hatched into a clone of the tadpole that donated the body cell.

This proved that thousands of genetically identical offspring could be spawned—at least from frogs—in the gleaming and bubbling beakers of a laboratory. Were test-tube human babies far away?

Indeed not. In July 1974 Dr. Douglas Bevis of Leeds University revealed that three children had been born to women whose ova were fertilized in a laboratory dish and then reimplanted in their wombs. Bevis refused to identify the children, but said that all are normal. Conceivably they are clones. The Bevis pronouncement has been called to question, and there is some doubt as to its specific veracity. No one, however, questioned its probability.

So now there seems no major obstacle to duplicating anybody in enormous quantities.

No doubt mass-production cloning will be tried first in animal husbandry, to breed the best cattle possible for meat. But why grow a whole steer when we can grow steaks instead? Nearly everyone has read of Alexis Carrel's chicken-heart culture, which grew meat for thirty-seven years and had to be constantly trimmed. The work on DNA has opened ways to control development so that any part of an organism can be nurtured separately.

This expertise will let scientists tinker with human heredity as they already do with microbe heredity, and manipulate genes to create new kinds of men. One obvious step is to grow human embryos outside the body and experiment on them. Exactly this is envisaged in a recent technical paper quoted in *Harper's:* "Laboratory embryos may some day be useful for assisting (*sic*) the hazards of new drugs and chemicals."

In other words, pharmaceutical companies can one day be testing new drugs on living human embryos in various stages of development, and watching with interest to see whether mutations and monstrosities appear. Some scientists are urging that this be made illegal immediately.

Popular sentiment seems likely to jump the other way.

Bereaved parents may yearn to buy a clone of their lost child. (Any leftover speck of the child's tissue might be used to breed the clone, since cells are neither "alive" nor "dead.") People who are unable to have children normally may press hard to keep test-tube pregnancies legal.

Then too, any woman who dreads the discomforts of pregnancy may be delighted to buy a tiny frozen embryo, and have it brought to birth outside her body. The embryo would, presumably, be sold with a guarantee that the resultant baby would be free of genetic defect. The buyer might even specify in advance the color of the baby's eyes and hair, its sex, its probable dimensions at maturity, and its probable intellectual attributes.

What kind of creatures will these babies become? Will they be humanoid instead of human? We know that important physical conditioning occurs in the uterus. And we feel fairly certain that infants are psychologically affected before birth by their mother's emotions and physiology.

Not every experiment succeeds, as the University of Alabama learned in trying to breed harmless microbes. If we attempt human cloning, what will we do with the live products of botched experiments? What will become of the near-successes and almost-persons?

A witch's brew is simmering in biological laboratories. Unless something unforeseen changes the trend, somewhere in the world there will soon be lab-made humans. "The work is easy to do and to conceal," says embryologist Robert G. Edwards of Cambridge. "If one nation prohibits it, others will permit it—leading either to smuggling of the work or emigration of people who do it."

And thus science imitates art and myth. Frankenstein's monster and the Golem are no longer altogether imaginary; we may see them on our streets any year now. Of all the monsters in the world's history, these may be the most magnificent or the most sinister.

BIBLIOGRAPHY

Augusta, J. and Burian, Z. *Prehistoric Sea Monsters*. London: Paul Hamlyn, 1964.

Bourne, Geoffrey. *The Gentle Giants*. New York: Putnam's, 1975.

Brewer, Ebenezer Cobham. *Brewer's Dictionary of Phrase & Fable* (revised). New York: Harper, 1947.

Byrne, Peter. *The Search for Bigfoot*. Washington: Acropolis, 1975.

Carrington, Richard. *Mermaids and Mastodons*. New York: Rinehart, 1957.

Cohen, Daniel. *A Modern Look at Monsters*. New York: Dodd Mead, 1970.

Costello, Peter. *In Search of Lake Monsters*. New York: Coward, McCann & Geoghegan, 1974.

Cronin, Edward W., Jr. "The Yeti," *Atlantic Monthly,* November 1975.

Dent, J. M. *Everyman Dictionary of Non-Classical Mythology*. New York: Dutton, 1952.

Desmond, Adrian. *The Hot-Blooded Dinosaurs*. New York: Dial, 1976.

Dinsdale, Timothy. *Monster Hunt*. Washington: Acropolis, 1972.

Eiseley, Loren. "The Time of Man," in *Light of the Past*. New York: American Heritage, 1965.

Eliot, Alexander. *Myths*. New York: McGraw-Hill, 1976.

Ellis, H. R. Davidson. *Gods and Myths of Northern Europe.* Harmondsworth: Penguin, 1964.

Emerson, B. K. "Geological Myths," *Science,* September 11, 1896.

Florescu, Radu. *In Search of Frankenstein.* New York: Warner, 1975.

Fossey, Dian. "Making Friends with Mountain Gorillas," *National Geographic,* January 1970.

Gaylin, Willard. "We Have the Awful Knowledge to Make Exact Copies of Human Beings," *New York Times Magazine,* March 5, 1972.

Gould, Rupert T. *The Loch Ness Monster and Others.* London: Bles, 1934.

Grumley, Michael. *There Are Giants in the Earth.* New York: Doubleday, 1974.

Hunter, Don and Dahinden, Rene. *Sasquatch.* Toronto: McClelland & Stewart, 1973.

Ley, Willy. *Dawn of Zoology.* Englewood Cliffs: Prentice-Hall, 1969.

Linnaean Society of New England. *Report Relative to a Large Marine Animal.* Boston: Linnaean Society, 1817.

Lum, Peter. *Fabulous Beasts.* London: Thames & Hudson, 1952.

MacCulloch, John A. and Gray, Louis H. *The Mythology of All Races.* New York: Cooper, 1922.

Mackal, Roy P. *The Monsters of Loch Ness.* Chicago: Swallow Press, 1976.

McNally, Raymond T. and Florescu, Radu. *In Search of Dracula.* New York: Warner, 1972.

Meade-Waldo, E. G. B. and Nicoll, Michael J. "Description of an Unknown Animal Seen at Sea off the Coast of Brazil," *Proceedings of the Zoological Society of London,* 1906.

Napier, John. *Bigfoot, the Yeti and Sasquatch in Myth and Reality.* New York: Dutton, 1973.

Natural History. "Here Come the Clones." February, 1975.

New Larousse Encyclopedia of Mythology. London: Hamlyn, 1976.

Oudemans, A. C. *The Great Sea Serpent*. London: Lonzac, 1892.

Ross, Nancy Wilson. "Sir Tashi and the Yeti," *Horizon,* Spring 1965.

Science Digest. "Tree Clones." April 1975.

Scott, David. "Closing in on the Loch Ness Monster," *Reader's Digest,* February 1967.

Slate, B. Ann and Berry, Alan. *Bigfoot.* New York: Bantam, 1976.

Smith, J. L. B., "The Second Coelacanth," *Nature,* Vol. 171. London, 1953.

Smith, Warren. *Strange Monsters and Madmen.* New York: Popular Library, 1969.

Soule, Gardner. *The Maybe Monsters.* New York: Putnam's, 1963.

Sterrett, J. R. S. "Vampires," *The Nation,* August 31, 1899.

Summers, Montague. *The Vampire: His Kith and Kin.* London: Routledge & Paul, 1928.

Voss, Gilbert. "Squids," *National Geographic,* March 1967.

Whyte, C. *More Than a Legend.* London: Hamilton, 1957.

Witchell, Nicholas. *The Loch Ness Story.* Baltimore: Penguin, 1975.

Wyckoff, Charles W. "Filming the Loch Ness Monster," *Filmmakers' Newsletter,* June 1976.

ABOUT THE AUTHOR

ALAN LANDSBURG is a successful film and television producer, heading up his own production company in Los Angeles, California. He was instrumental in bringing the von Däniken phenomenon to the attention of the American public through TV by producing "In Search of Ancient Astronauts." Alan Landsburg is also the author of *In Search of Ancient Mysteries* and *The Outer Space Connection*. He is currently working on a weekly television series, "In Search Of . . .," which has been on the air since September, 1976. *In Search of Myths and Monsters* and five other books on extraterrestrials, magic and witchcraft, lost civilizations, strange phenomena and people, are based on this series.

OTHER WORLDS
OTHER REALITIES

In fact and fiction, these extraordinary books bring the fascinating world of the supernatural down to earth from ancient astronauts and black magic to witchcraft, voodoo and mysticism—these books look at other worlds and examine other realities.

Bantam Book Catalog

Here's your up-to-the-minute listing of every book currently available from Bantam.

This easy-to-use catalog is divided into categories and contains over 1400 titles by your favorite authors.

So don't delay—take advantage of this special opportunity to increase your reading pleasure.

Just send us your name and address and 25¢ (to help defray postage and handling costs).